# ASSURANCE
## OF
# SALVATION

*Lucy Bassett*
*January 2001*

# Hans K. LaRondelle

**Pacific Press® Publishing Association**
Nampa, Idaho
Oshawa, Ontario, Canada

Edited by David C. Jarnes
Cover designed by Dennis Ferree
Cover art by Justinen Creative Group

The accuracy of the quotations is the responsibility of the author.

Unless otherwise noted, all Scripture quotations are taken from the New International Version.

LaRondelle, Hans K.
    Assurance of salvation  /  Hans K. LaRondelle
      p.   cm.
    ISBN 0-8163-1712-7
    1. Assurance (Theology)—Biblical teaching.  2. Salvation—Biblical teaching.  I. Title.
    BS680.A86L38   1999
    234—dc21                                                    99-16208
                                                                      CIP

99 00 01 02 03 • 5 4 3 2 1

# *Contents*

# *Introduction*

The quest for certainty plays an indispensable role in Christian faith and religion. It was the search for assurance of salvation that gave rise to the Protestant Reformation in the sixteenth century. In reaction, the Council of Trent decreed in 1547 that no Christian "can know with the certainty of faith, which cannot be subject to error, that he has obtained the grace of God," except by "a special revelation from God."[1]

At the foundation of the Protestant faith lies the believers' trust in God's assurance that He has accepted them. The beginning of the Heidelberg Catechism of 1563 expresses this truth impressively:

> Q. *What is your only comfort, in life and in death?*
> A. That I belong—body and soul, in life and in death—not to myself but to my faithful Savior, Jesus Christ, who at the cost of his own blood has fully paid for all my sins and has completely freed me from the dominion of the devil. . . . Therefore, by his Holy Spirit, he also assures me of eternal life, and makes me wholeheartedly willing and ready from now on to live for him.[2]

Ever facing the possibility of persecution, believers would not have been able to stand the test of faith if they had doubts about Jesus and their relation to Him. Here we see the essential difference between Roman Catholic faith and historic Protestant faith—the firm assurance of personal salvation here and now! Unfortunately, seventeenth-century Protestant scholasticism largely lost this personal assurance; trust in belief systems replaced personal faith in Jesus. But certainty of dogmatic truths won't suffice for Christians. They need also the certainty of salvation.

Faith in the promises God has given in the gospel brings its own certainty. This assurance comes not as some special revelation's addition to faith but as the believer stands firmly on God's promises. Herman Bavinck said it well:

> This certainty [of faith] is contained in faith from the outset and in time organically issues from it. Faith *is* certainty and as such excludes all doubt. . . . Certainty is an essential characteristic of faith; it is inseparable from it and belongs to its nature.[3]

Jesus Himself illustrated the nature of saving faith with a dramatic story from the Old Testament. He told Nicodemus:

> "Just as Moses lifted up the snake in the desert, so the Son of Man must be lifted up, that everyone who believes in him may have eternal life" (John 3:14, 15).

Moses had invited the dying Israelites to look at a bronze snake raised on a pole, telling them, "Anyone who is bitten can look at it and live" (Num. 21:8). Their act of looking showed their faith in God's promise. "They lived because they believed God's word, and trusted in the means provided for their recovery. So the sinner may look to Christ, and live."[4]

Believers become sure of their salvation solely through faith in Jesus. Faith itself is not our savior but the "hand" by which we accept Jesus' gift of salvation. So our certainty doesn't come *from* our faith but *through* our faith in Jesus. Consequently, the Christian's assurance of salvation does not rest on human reasoning or feeling but exclusively on the trustworthy promise of God. To forgiven sinners, the Spirit of God Himself "testifies with our spirit that we are God's children" (Rom. 8:16).

---

1. In J. Leith, *Creeds of the Churches* (Atlanta: J. Knox Press, 1977), 414, 422.

2. In A. C. Cochrane, *Reformed Confessions of the Sixteenth Century* (Philadelphia: The Westminster Press, 1966), 305.

3. Herman Bavinck, *The Certainty of Faith* (St. Catharines, Ontario: Paideia Press, 1980), 85, 86.

4. E. G. White, *Patriarchs and Prophets*, 431.

*Chapter 1*

# The Foundation
# of Assurance

We obtain assurance of salvation when we hear God speak to our hearts and minds. He speaks to us primarily through the Scriptures and through the Holy Spirit.

In the beginning, God spoke directly to Adam and Eve. Later He spoke to the patriarchs and prophets of Israel. Moses held a unique place among them—because, God said, " 'With him I speak face to face, clearly and not in riddles' " (Num. 12:8). Consequently, Moses' writings became the touchstone for testing the continuing gift of prophecy. Israel accepted the writings of the prophets as divinely inspired when they found them to be in harmony with the Torah, the teachings of Moses (see Deut. 18:15-20).

Jesus appealed to Moses' writings on the assumption that they possessed divine authority and trustworthiness (see Matt. 19:4, 5; Luke 20:37). He also accepted the book of Psalms as divinely inspired and as part of the Torah (Matt. 22:43, 44; John 10:34). And He saw His mission as fulfilling the Messianic prophecies of Isaiah (see Luke 4:17-21; 22:37).

The letter to the Hebrews not only recognizes the previous revelations of God to Israel but also acknowledges the new disclosure of the same God by Christ Jesus:

In the past God spoke to our forefathers through the prophets at many times and in various ways, but in these last days he has spoken to us by his Son, whom he appointed heir of all things, and through whom he made the universe (Heb. 1:1, 2).

## The normative testimony of Jesus

The New Testament Gospels contain the canonical or normative "testimony of Jesus." He declared: " 'The one who comes from heaven is above all. He testifies to what he has seen and heard, but no one accepts his testimony' " (John 3:31, 32). Note what He said next: " *'The man who has accepted it has certified that God is truthful.* For the one whom God has sent speaks the words of God, for God gives the Spirit without limit' " (John 3:33, 34, emphasis supplied).

The book of Acts and the apostolic letters explain the significance of Jesus' life, death, and teachings, which, in turn, represent the legal testimony of God to all nations (Matt. 24:14). Paul identified the source of these books. He declared that his gospel message was not of human origin: "I did not receive it from any man, nor was I taught it; rather, I received it by revelation from Jesus Christ" (Gal. 1:12). On this basis he stated: "Here is a trustworthy saying that deserves full acceptance: Christ Jesus came into the world to save sinners—of whom I am the worst" (1 Tim. 1:15). He thanked the church in Thessalonica that they had received his gospel message "not as the word of men, but as it actually is, *the word of God, which is at work in you who believe*" (1 Thess. 2:13).

Paul understood what prevented his fellow Jews from accepting Jesus as the Messiah of Israel. He said that a "veil" covered their minds when they read the old covenant Scriptures: "It has not been removed, because only in Christ is it taken away. . . . But whenever anyone turns to the Lord, the veil is taken away" (2 Cor. 3:14-16). This statement discloses that to understand the Old Testament fully, we need the New Testament testimony of Jesus. The Old Testament finds its center in the Messianic prophecies, as Jesus Himself taught (see John 5:39, 40, 46).

The book of Revelation brings the final testimony of Jesus that the New Testament contains: " 'I, Jesus, have sent my angel to give you this testimony for the churches' " (Rev. 22:16). A direct declaration from the throne of God guaranteed its promises for the future:

" 'I am making everything new!' Then he said, 'Write this down, for these words are trustworthy and true' " (Rev. 21:5). The conclusion of the Apocalypse warns us not to add or to take away anything from this revelation of divine truth that closes the canon of Scripture (Rev. 22:18, 19).

Christians accept both the Word of God that came through the prophets and the testimony of Jesus as one progressive testimony conveyed through two Testaments (Heb. 1:1, 2). On this platform of Scripture all followers of Jesus stand united in Him. To believe God means to believe His Word. To trust the God of Israel means to trust Jesus and His gospel promises.

Paul acknowledged the sufficiency of Scripture when he wrote to Timothy: "You have known the holy Scriptures, which are able to make you wise for salvation through faith in Christ Jesus" (2 Tim. 3:15). Here we notice that the Scriptures are sufficient to teach us the way of salvation. That is the primary purpose of the Bible. Paul added that it also serves to rebuke, correct, and train in righteousness, "so that the man of God may be thoroughly equipped for every good work" (2 Tim. 3:16, 17). This means that the Bible is sufficient for salvation and sanctification. Consequently, the apostle warned the churches: "Do not go beyond what is written" (1 Cor. 4:6).

The influential Belgic Confession of Faith of 1561 represents the Protestant faith accurately. It declares in Article 7: "We believe that these Holy Scriptures fully contain the will of God, and that whatsoever man ought to believe unto salvation, is sufficiently taught therein."[1] Ellen G. White stated this faith with unsurpassed clarity:

> In His word, God has committed to men the knowledge necessary for salvation. The Holy Scriptures are to be accepted as an authoritative, infallible revelation of His will. They are the standard of character, the revealer of doctrines, and the test of experience.[2]

This means that the Bible gives a sure knowledge of God, of Christ, and of salvation.

## The clarity of Scripture

It is crucially important that we believe in Scripture's clarity regarding the way of salvation and of sanctification. Here many stumble, thinking we must have extrabiblical authorities to tell us what the Bible says. Such a belief makes the human conscience vulnerable to enslavement to ecclesiastical institutions and traditions or to human philosophies.

We need to realize that in both Testaments God addressed His words to the common people. Moses declared to the Israelites that they should not assume that God's word was far away from them: "No, the word is very near you; it is in your mouth and in your heart so you may obey it" (Deut. 30:14). Foundational to Israel's religion was the belief that God's words are clear and thus require the response of a faithful obedience. Israel's worship songs expressed this belief:

Your word is a lamp to my feet and a light for my path. . . .
The unfolding of your words gives light; it gives understanding to the simple (Ps. 119:105, 130).

Similarly, in the New Testament, Peter urged all Christian believers to pay close attention to the prophetic word of God:

We have the word of the prophets made more certain, and you will do well to pay attention to it, as to a light shining in a dark place, until the day dawns and the morning star rises in your hearts (2 Pet. 1:19).

However, Scripture is clear to faith alone; to grasp its deep meaning, readers must have the illumination of the Spirit of God. Paul explained: "The man without the Spirit does not accept the things that come from the Spirit of God, for they are foolishness to him, and he cannot understand them, because they are spiritually discerned" (1 Cor. 2:14).

The Protestant Reformers discovered that God had not intended the Bible to be a book of laws and regulations that had to be interpreted by a church authority and to be adapted to changing cultures. By listening carefully to the words of Scripture, they heard the voice of the living God speaking to their hearts with the clear message of His redeeming grace. They no longer understood Scripture as an abstract system of intellectual truths but as the personal voice of God that evoked faith in their hearts and placed them in His immediate presence.

The authority of Scripture, then, became the authority of God Himself. And Scripture became the source of a living faith and hope. One author explains: "In the religious situation of redemption of the man *coram Deo* [before God's presence] there is no . . . authority between God and man other than the authority of His living word."[3] Believers who have been touched by the Lord Himself through Scripture experience an absolute certainty of faith and grace. They regard the revelation of God's will in Scripture as the voice of God speaking directly to them, assuring them of His forgiveness and acceptance.

The Protestant Reformers expressed their conviction of the clarity of Scripture in the confessional statement: *sola scriptura*. In essence this phrase meant that *Scripture is its own interpreter*. It expresses the experience of faith that God is His own best expositor. It also declares that Scripture alone makes humanity's position before God sufficiently clear. The Reformers likened the Bible to the sun that needs no light from the earth. Scripture radiates its own light of truth and needs no candle of illumination from human philosophy or ecclesiastical authority. Scripture alone determines the content of saving faith. It has this clarity because it is the living Word of God through which God confers His grace on the hearer.

Calvin stressed the importance of the unity of Scripture and the Spirit of God for the clear understanding of the biblical message.

Indeed, the Word of God is like the sun, shining upon all those to whom it is proclaimed, but with no effect among the blind. Now, all of us are blind by nature in this respect. Accordingly, it cannot penetrate into our minds unless the Spirit, as the inner teacher, through his illumination makes entry for it.[4]

Our certainty of faith and of salvation depends on the clarity and truthfulness of the Word of God—of the gospel of Jesus Christ in particular. Ellen G. White explained the importance of our attitude toward the Bible:

> Only he who receives the Scriptures as the voice of God speaking to himself is a true learner. He trembles at the word; for to him it is a living reality. He opens his understanding and his heart to receive it.[5]

## The efficacy of Scripture

The Reformers recognized that the Word of God is the instrument of the Holy Spirit. They confessed that the connection of the Word and the Spirit is of critical importance for the testing of the Spirit, because many false spirits claimed divine authority (see 1 John 4:1; 2:18). In this respect Paul called the Word of God "*the sword of the Spirit*" (Eph. 6:17, emphasis supplied). This metaphor indicates the indissoluble relation between the Word and the Spirit. Earlier, Jesus had said: " 'The Spirit gives life; the flesh counts for nothing. The words I have spoken to you are spirit and they are life' " (John 6:63). Jesus' words apply also to the biblical message, to the preaching of the Word of God. Ellen White explained this:

> Through the Scriptures the Holy Spirit speaks to the mind, and impresses truth upon the heart. Thus He exposes error, and expels it from the soul. It is by the Spirit of truth, working through the word of God, that Christ subdues His chosen people to Himself.[6]

Through the working of the Holy Spirit, the Word of God reveals the distinction between truth and error and convicts sinners of their guilt before God—especially of the sin of rejecting the Son of God. Jesus said this is the primary function of the Spirit: " 'When he comes, he will convict the world of guilt in regard to sin and righteousness and judgment: *in regard to sin, because men do not believe in me*' " (John 16:8, 9, emphasis added).

The letter to the Hebrews portrays the effectiveness of the Word of God in the believer, who needs to enter the rest of God:

> The word of God is living and active. Sharper than any double-edged sword, it penetrates even to dividing soul and spirit, joints and marrow; it judges the thoughts and attitudes of the heart. Nothing in all creation is hidden from God's sight. Everything is uncovered and laid bare before the eyes of him to whom we must give account (Heb. 4:12, 13).*

So, the Word of God can penetrate deeply into the human psyche. William Lane explains that it can

> reach into the deepest recesses of the human personality. . . . The discrimination of the heart's thoughts and intentions entails a sifting process that exhibits the penetrative and unmasking potency of the word. . . . Exposure to the word of Scripture entails exposure to God himself.[7]

Hebrews 4:12 also warns us that the history of Israel reveals that the Word of God possesses the power to fulfill its own promises and curses.

Both Luther and Calvin saw the danger of separating the Word from the Spirit. They recognized that both Roman Catholics and extremists among the Anabaptists were making one-sided appeals to the Holy Spirit to justify their dogmatic positions. So the Reformers stressed that the Spirit operates only with and through the Scriptures—never against it. They compared the union of Scripture and the Spirit with the inseparable union of light and heat in the sun. Lennart Pinomaa summed up Luther's view:

> In fact, it [the Bible] is an incarnation of the Spirit. As the rays of the sun have heat as well as light, so the outward Word

---

*The reference to the living "word of God" in Hebrews 4 is drawn from God's warning in Psalm 95:7-11 (see Heb. 3:7-4:7).

includes the Spirit. The Word is followed by the Spirit. This order must not be changed. First the Word, then the Spirit.[8]

Calvin's formulation of the union of Word and Spirit as "the inward testimony of the Spirit" became well known:

As God alone is a fit witness of himself in his Word, so also the Word will not find acceptance in men's hearts before it is sealed by the inward testimony of the Spirit. The same Spirit, therefore, who has spoken through the mouths of the prophets must penetrate into our hearts to persuade us that they faithfully proclaimed what had been divinely commanded [Isa. 59:21 quoted].[9]

This perceptive insight allowed Calvin to conclude that we don't derive our belief in God's Word through our own judgment nor through the church doctrine that Scripture is from God. "*Above human judgment we affirm with utter certainty (just as if we were gazing upon the majesty of God himself) that it has flowed to us from the very mouth of God by the ministry of men.*"[10]

God unites and preserves His chosen people on the platform of the Bible and the Bible alone. The book of Revelation emphasizes repeatedly that the true church is built on the word (or commandments) of God and the testimony (or faith) of Jesus (see Rev. 1:2, 9; 6:9; 12:17; 14:12; 19:10; 20:4). And Ellen White affirmed: "God will have a people upon the earth to maintain the Bible, and the Bible only, as the standard of all doctrines and the basis of all reforms."[11]

The people of God need this biblical foundation of assurance. More than that, they need the assurance of salvation that comes as the fruit of accepting the living voice of God through the Scriptures.

---

1. In A. C. Cochrane, ed.; *Reformed Confessions of the Sixteenth Century* (Philadelphia: The Westminster Press, 1966), 192.
2. *The Great Controversy*, vii.

3. H. W. Rossouw, *Klaarheid en Interpretasie* (Amsterdam: J. van Campen NV, 1963), 159. My translation.

4. *Institutes of the Christian Religion*, bk. III, ch. 2, sec. 34.

5. *Christ's Object Lessons*, 59.

6. *The Desire of Ages*, 671.

7. William Lane, *Hebrews 1-8*, Word Biblical Commentary, vol. 47a (Dallas, Tex.: Word Books, 1991), 103.

8. Lennart Pinomaa, *Faith Victorious* (Philadelphia: Fortress Press, 1963), 103.

9. *Institutes*, bk. I, ch. 7, sec. 4.

10. *Institutes*, bk. I, ch. 7, sec. 5; emphasis added.

11. E. G. White, *The Great Controversy*, 595.

*Chapter 2*

# The Person of Christ: Our Assurance

While the Bible is the foundation of our assurance of faith, it is in the person of Jesus that we find our assurance of salvation.

Jesus noticed that the rabbis and Pharisees sought their assurance of salvation in Scripture—particularly, in conforming their lives to its laws and regulations. He observed that they were surface readers of the Bible and did not penetrate to its redemptive message. They even misapplied the Messianic prophecies, believing them to foretell a coming political figure. So Jesus alerted the Jewish leaders to their fundamental misconception:

"You pore over the scriptures, for you imagine that you will find eternal life in them. All the time they give their testimony to me, but you are not willing to come to me to have real life!" (John 5:39, 40, J. B. Phillips).

Here is a lesson for all time. Our assurance of salvation is not anchored in a book but in a Person—in a personal relationship to Jesus, the Messiah of prophecy.

To obtain this assurance of salvation, we must have a correct view of Jesus, the Christ of the Scriptures. Ellen G. White explained the necessity of an unbiased insight:

While the Jews desired the advent of the Messiah, they had no true conception of His mission. They did not seek redemption of sin, but deliverance from the Romans. They looked for the Messiah to come as a conqueror, to break the oppressor's power, and exalt Israel to universal dominion. Thus the way was prepared for them to reject the Savior. . . . They interpreted prophecy in accordance with their selfish desires.[1]

To receive assurance of salvation, we must know more than the Bible and its promises. We must know the Author and Center of Scripture: Jesus Himself. How is this possible? Peter wrote:

Though you have not seen him, you love him; and even though you do not see him now, you believe in him and are filled with an inexpressible and glorious joy, for you are receiving the goal of your faith, the salvation of your souls (1 Pet. 1:8, 9).

Peter says that Christians have come to *love* Jesus and experience the *joy* of a present salvation. This spiritual joy leaves no room for doubt. The apostle explains that this assurance of salvation comes through faith in the risen Christ. He enlarges this assurance by stating "in his [God's] great mercy he has given us new birth into a living hope through the resurrection of Christ from the dead, and into an inheritance that can never perish, spoil or fade" (1 Pet. 1:3, 4). His words indicate that assurance of salvation cannot be abstracted from Jesus' person and from our personal communion with Him.

Peter declared that the Hebrew prophets searched for this joy and certainty by studying the Messianic promises (see 1 Pet. 1:10, 11). But their view of the two stages of the Messiah's mission was obscured. Only after His resurrection could Jesus explain the meaning of His sufferings in the light of the fulfillment of prophecy:

"Did not the Christ have to suffer these things and then enter his glory?" And beginning with Moses and all the Prophets, he explained to them what was said in all the Scriptures concerning himself (Luke 24:26, 27).

The central message of the Old Testament is not about Israel but about Jesus. And while the Old Testament teaches us *what* the Messiah will do, it is the New Testament that teaches us *who* the Messiah is. The most critical question we face is how deeply we are convinced that Jesus of Nazareth is the Messiah of prophecy. After asking His disciples what other people were saying about Him, Jesus asked, " 'What about you? Who do you say I am?' " (Matt. 16:15). He pronounced a blessing on Peter when he replied, *" 'You are the Christ [Messiah], the Son of the living God' "* (Matt. 16:16, emphasis supplied).

What does this confession of faith in Jesus' messiahship mean?

## The Christ of Scripture

To understand Jesus' redemptive work, we need to know His person. While we cannot separate Jesus' mission from His person, we must realize that it is His divinity that gives eternal and universal value to His work. G. C. Berkouwer perceived it well: "It is quite impossible rightly to understand the work of Christ without revelation, that is, without understanding that it is God acting in Jesus Christ."[2] To know Jesus we must know Scripture; Jesus comes to us as the fulfillment of the Messianic prophecies and He wants us to believe in Him on that basis. His words make this quite evident. He said to the Jews: " 'If you believed Moses, you would believe me, for he wrote about me. But since you do not believe what he wrote, how are you going to believe what I say?' " (John 5:46, 47).

Even more striking is the method Jesus used to convince the downcast disciples on the road to Emmaus of His divine messiahship. He did not perform a miracle. Instead, He deliberately "kept [them] from recognizing him" and gave them an extended Bible study on the Old Testament's Messianic prophecies and types (see Luke 24:16, 27). Jesus' lesson on His fulfillment of the Old Testament assured them of His divine person and mission. When their eyes were opened and they recognized Him, they said to each other: " 'Were not our hearts burning within us while he talked with us on the road and opened the Scriptures to us?' " (Luke 24:32).

Soon afterward the risen Lord appeared among the apostles who were assembled in Jerusalem. When He had shown them His hands and feet and had eaten with them to convince them of the reality of His resurrection, He said to them: " 'Everything must be fulfilled that is written about me in the Law of Moses, the Prophets and the Psalms.' Then he opened their minds so they could understand the Scriptures" (Luke 24:44, 45).

The assurance of Jesus' deity comes to the student of the prophetic Word through the quiet conviction of the Spirit of God and a "burning" of the heart. This joyful assurance is built not on some passing feeling or wondrous event but on the Christ of Scripture. Faith and joy like that the disciples knew is grounded firmly on the reliable and trustworthy Word of God—on "it is written"!

So, the gospel of salvation is founded on the fulfillment of the prophetic Word of God, and the New Testament Gospels are the wondrous fulfillment of the Old Testament promises of redemption. The gospel of Christ makes a Christian book of the Old Testament. Berkouwer observed that the Gospels view Jesus as "the fulfillment of the entire Old Testament. . . . [This conclusion] is evident from all the data we face—not a few incidental and arbitrary illustrations but a comprehensive testimony pointing to and converging on the coming Redeemer Jesus Christ."[3] This amazing fact demonstrates convincingly that all Holy Scripture proclaims Jesus' divine messiahship and that all the Bible is a Christ-centered book.

## The deity of Christ

Jesus claimed not only that the Father in heaven sent Him but also that from eternity He was one with God the Father. He expressed His divine self-consciousness by announcing that He is the One who gives the divine rest our souls can enjoy: " 'Come to me, all you who are weary and burdened, and I will give you rest. Take my yoke upon you and learn from me, for I am gentle and humble in heart, and you will find rest for your souls' " (Matt. 11:28, 29). In this redemptive way Jesus fulfilled the divine promises of spiritual rest the Hebrew Scriptures contain:

My soul finds rest in God alone; my salvation comes from him. He alone is my rock and my salvation (Ps. 62:1).

> Be at rest once more, O my soul, for the LORD has been good to you (Ps. 116:7).
>
> In that day the Root of Jesse [of the royal house of David] will stand as a banner for the peoples; the nations will rally to him, and his place of rest will be glorious (Isa. 11:10).

Jesus—in the stead of God—offers this Messianic rest, the rest of grace, to all people. Consequently, our relation to Jesus as the unique Son of God determines our relation to God. But these two persons do not compete for honor and glory. Jesus consistently recognized His union with the Father. In His high-priestly prayer, He said: " 'Now this is eternal life: that they may know you, the only true God, and Jesus Christ, whom you have sent' " (John 17:3, emphasis supplied). These words hold profound significance for our assurance of salvation. They indicate that those who know Jesus know God! And knowing God and His Son brings the assurance of eternal life. How diligently, then, we should seek to know Jesus truly, to know Him heart to heart!

The essential unity of the Father and the Son allows the Father to assign judgment, the prerogative of the Creator, to the Son: " 'Moreover, the Father judges no one, but has entrusted all judgment to the Son, that all may honor the Son just as they honor the Father. He who does not honor the Son does not honor the Father, who sent him' " (John 5:22, 23, emphasis supplied). Heaven acknowledges Jesus' claim to equal honor with God the Father. "Every creature in heaven and on earth and under the earth" joins in the acclamation: " 'To him who sits on the throne and to the Lamb be praise and honor and glory and power for ever and ever!' " (Rev. 5:13).

Could Jesus receive such divine honor and glory if He were not equal to God? How could He be worshiped by "every creature" if He were Himself a creature?

Jesus knew that He had possessed divine glory before His incarnation. He prayed, " 'Father, glorify me in your presence with *the glory I had with you before the world began. . . .* I want those you have given me to be with me where I am, and to see my glory, *the glory you have given me because you loved me before the creation of the world'* " (John 17:5, 24, emphasis added).

Jer 15 :16

thy words found,

√ I. did eat them

## Jesus' subordination to the Father

Near the end of His ministry on earth Jesus said " 'the Father is greater than I' " (John 14:28). How shall we understand that statement?

It is the historical setting that determines the meaning of the superiority of the Father. Jesus spoke of the completion of His state of Incarnation and suffering and announced His coming entrance into glory in His Father's house (John 14:2, 28). Then He contrasted His present humiliation with His impending exaltation. The Father to whom He is going was greater than the Mediator in His human likeness (see Phil. 2:6-8; Heb. 5:8). The Father is now—while Jesus is in His state of subordination to Him—superior to Jesus.

Berkouwer comments that this duality of Jesus' divine person and His submission to the Father "does not imply a conflict between his deity and his subordination as Mediator: his having come and his being sent."[4] A little later that same night Jesus referred to His being a servant of the Father and said that He would soon be greater than He was at that point. When He had fulfilled His current task, He would receive again the glory He possessed before He came to the world (John 17:5).

John declared Jesus' deity: "No one has ever seen God, but *God the One and Only, who is at the Father's side*, has made him known" (John 1:18, emphasis added). Paul also proclaimed His divinity: "Who, being in very nature God, did not consider equality with God something to be grasped" (Phil. 2:6). "*In Christ all the fullness of the Deity lives in bodily form*" (Col. 2:9, emphasis supplied).

Jesus asserted His essential unity with God: " 'I and the Father are one' "; " 'Anyone who has seen me has seen the Father' " (John 10:30; 14:9). No wonder that He can offer life eternal to those who believe in Him! " 'No one can come to me unless the Father who sent me draws him, and *I will raise him up at the last day*' "; " 'All that the Father gives me will come to me, and *whoever comes to me I will never drive away*' " (John 6:44, 37, emphasis supplied). The Father fully endorses Jesus' desire to save for eternity all who come to Him: " 'This is the will of him who sent me, that I shall lose none of all that he has given me, but raise them up at the last day' " (John 6:39).

The soul does not possess eternal life as a natural attribute; it receives this gift only "at the last day," when the Creator/Redeemer transforms it. Three times Jesus demonstrated that He was able to raise the dead to life (see Luke 7:14, 15; 8:53-56; John 11:38-44). His raising of Lazarus made the point that Martha's faith in the Jewish doctrine of the resurrection no longer sufficed. He wanted more than a profession of orthodox faith in the resurrection (see Dan. 12:2). Jesus disclosed to Martha God's new truth: " *'I am the resurrection and the life*. He who believes in me will live, even though he dies; and whoever lives and believes in me will never die.' " Then He asked, " 'Do you believe this?' " (John 11:25, 26, emphasis added). Here we see the advance from Judaism to Christian faith. Here Jesus makes His most amazing claim. He not only offers forgiveness of sins but also guarantees life eternal, the resurrection from the dead.

John summarized the gospel in this succinct assurance of salvation: "*He who has the Son has life*; he who does not have the Son of God does not have life" (1 John 5:12, emphasis added). What a wonderful assurance in Christ! When the doubting Thomas saw the risen Lord and touched His hands and feet, he confessed in awe: " 'My Lord and my God!' " (John 20:28). So Ellen White is justified in stating: "In Christ is life, original, unborrowed, underived. . . . The divinity of Christ is the believer's assurance of eternal life."[5]

## The "I AM" sayings of Jesus

The fourth Gospel records a number of "I am" statements that Jesus made. Jews find these statements disconcerting because they directly touch the sacred name of God. One scholar explains: "In Exodus 3:14 the name YHWH is connected with the verb form 'I am ( *'ehyeh*),' which is understood as a proper name and is repeated three times: 'I AM WHO I AM,' and 'I AM has sent . . .' "[6] Jesus' use of the absolute "I Am" (*Ego Eimi*) to describe Himself was quite provocative. By pronouncing this phrase, Jesus was virtually identifying Himself with the sacred name that was revealed to Moses at the bush (Exod. 3:14, 15). This adds new meaning to His claim that He had made known the "name" of God to His disciples (John 17:6, 26, NRSV).

It is also significant that Isaiah used the phrase *'Ani Hu* ["I Am

He"] many times to refer to the God of Israel. This phrase signifies that Yahweh alone is the living God (see Isa. 47:8, 10) and that He is the Redeemer and Sustainer of Israel (see Isa. 41:4; 43:10-13, 25; 46:4). In short, God's Old-Testament self-designations, "I AM" and "I Am He," indicate His redemptive work for Israel and *"constituted a promise or reassurance of salvation to Israel."*[7]

Jesus expressed His divine authority and redemptive mission in His "I Am" statements. Some of them indicate specifically His saving work: for instance, " 'I am the bread of life' " (John 6:35); " 'I am the light of the world' " (John 8:12); and " 'I am the good shepherd. The good shepherd lays down his life for the sheep' " (John 10:11). In other statements Jesus used no predicate: for example, " 'When you have lifted up the Son of Man, then you will know that *I am He* [*Ego Eimi*], and that I do nothing on my own authority but speak as the Father taught me' " (John 8:28, RSV); and " 'Truly, truly, I say to you, before Abraham was, *I am* [*Ego Eimi*]' " (John 8:58, RSV). In these last two declarations, Jesus used the phrase "I am" in an absolute sense—that is, as complete in itself. He even made it a test of faith. He said: " 'I told you that you would die in your sins; for you will die in your sins unless you believe that *I am he* [*Ego Eimi*]' " (John 8:24, RSV).

The meaning of Jesus' words is not self-evident. It must be disclosed to faith and be appropriated by faith. Only after Jesus' death and resurrection could the full significance be seen (John 13:19). Jesus developed this significance when He said, " 'He who receives me receives him who sent me' " (John 13:20). Here we find a key to understanding the absolute "I AM": to receive Him is to receive the Father.

Philip Harner comments:

> It indicates the unity of the Father and the Son, a unity that only Jesus can speak of during his lifetime but which others will be able to perceive in faith after his glorification and within the context of the continuing mission of his followers.[8]

The Jews of Jesus' time understood that He was claiming deity when He called Himself the "I AM." They rejected His claim as a blasphemy and started to stone Him (John 8:59; 10:31-33). Jesus insisted, however, that He was the I AM before Abraham came into existence (John 8:58). He clarified His unity with the Father in terms of a mutual indwelling: " 'that you may know and understand that the Father is in me, and I am in the Father' " (John 10:38). Here Jesus disclosed that distinct persons exist within the Godhead in a mutual interrelationship. Their unity is revealed as a dynamic communion in which both Persons are committed to saving humanity for all eternity.

John's Apocalypse concludes with a profound reassurance of Jesus' faithfulness to the plan of redemption: " 'I am the Alpha and the Omega, the First and the Last, the Beginning and the End' " (Rev. 22:13). In Revelation 1:8, John applied these sacred titles to God the Father. At the conclusion of the book, he applied them in full force also to our divine Lord and Redeemer, Jesus Christ.

Scripture portrays Jesus as fully divine. He has all the authority and all the power required to save us for eternity. That's why when we rest in faith in Him, we can find full assurance of our salvation.

---

1. E. G. White, *The Desire of Ages*, 29, 30.
2. G. C. Berkouwer, *The Person of Christ* (Grand Rapids, Mich.: Eerdmans, 1973), 106.
3. Ibid., 117.
4. Ibid., 188.
5. E. G. White, *The Desire of Ages*, 530.
6. P. B. Harner, *The "I Am" of the Fourth Gospel* (Philadelphia: Facet Books, 1970), 16.
7. Ibid., 10.
8. Ibid., 39.

*Chapter 3*

# The Work of Christ: Our Assurance

We cannot know Jesus apart from His redemptive work for humankind. The name *Christ* itself signifies His title and authority as God's "Anointed One," meaning that He was equipped with the fullness of God's Spirit to accomplish a special mission for God.

The Messianic prophecies of the Hebrew prophets focus primarily on heralding the coming of this divine emissary. The following predictions of Isaiah stand out in their clarity:

> A shoot will come up from the stump of Jesse [King David's father]; from his roots a Branch will bear fruit. The Spirit of the LORD will rest on him—the Spirit of wisdom and of understanding, the Spirit of counsel and of power, the Spirit of knowledge and of the fear of the LORD—and he will delight in the fear of the LORD (Isa. 11:1, 2).

> The Spirit of the Sovereign Lord is on me, because the LORD has anointed me to preach good news to the poor. He has sent me to bind up the brokenhearted, to proclaim freedom for the captives and release from darkness for the prisoners, to proclaim the year of the LORD's favor and the day of vengeance of our God, to comfort all who mourn (Isa. 61:1, 2).

The Sabbath after Jesus had been anointed with the fullness of God's Spirit at His baptism (see Matt. 3:16, 17; Acts 10:38), He announced that the prophecy of Isaiah 61 had found its fulfillment in Him (see Luke 4:16-21). His primary mission was not to preach or to heal people but to conquer Satan and his power over humankind. His message regarding the reign—the kingdom—of God encompassed a spiritual struggle with the fundamental problem of evil. He had to deal with this root of all evil before anyone could benefit from His ministry. That's why the Spirit led Him into the wilderness to meet the temptations of the devil (Luke 4:1-13).

George E. Ladd explains the decisive importance of the problem of evil:

> The demonic is absolutely essential in understanding Jesus' interpretation of the picture of sin and of man's need for the Kingdom of God. Man is in bondage to a personal power stronger than himself. At the very heart of our Lord's mission is the need of rescuing men from bondage to the satanic kingdom and of bringing them into the sphere of God's Kingdom.[1]

The kingdom of God entered the world in Christ Jesus. He demonstrated His liberating power by delivering the demon-possessed, explaining: " 'If I drive out demons by the Spirit of God, then the kingdom of God *has* come upon you' " (Matt. 12:28, emphasis added). Jesus declared that He had "bound" the strong one (Matt. 12:29). By this metaphor of "binding" Satan, He indicated that He has restrained the power of evil. Satan has not been rendered powerless, but his overmastering power has been broken. He has fallen from his place of dominion over humanity, though his destruction waits for the end of the age (Luke 10:18; Rev. 20:10). So, where Jesus is, there is the kingdom of God.[*]

Jesus saw His mission as restoring the communion between God and humanity through representing God's redemptive love. His mission to save the lost included the past, present and future. That mis-

---

[*]See Luke 17:20, 21. The phrase *entos humôn* can mean either "within you" or "in your midst."

sion encompassed the whole world. Even Israel, the chosen people, were like lost sheep without a caring shepherd. That's why Ezekiel's Messianic prophecy promised the coming of the true Shepherd (Ezek. 34:11-24). Jesus told the repentant Zacchaeus: " '*Today* salvation has come to this house. . . . For the Son of Man came to seek and to save what was lost' " (Luke 19:9, 10, emphasis added). In this statement, He was claiming to fulfill Ezekiel's promise.

Notice that the joyful news is *present* salvation, salvation *today*! Jesus' parables of the lost sheep, the lost coin, and the lost son in Luke 15 also describe this present salvation. And we particularly see the presence of Messianic salvation in Jesus' miracles of healing from illnesses and resurrection from death itself (Luke 4:38-41; 5:12-26; 8:53-56; John 11). He taught that these deliverances evidenced the presence of the Messiah and of His salvation (see Matt. 11:4, 5).

Undoubtedly, however, the greatest gift of the Messiah was the forgiveness of sins. God alone can give this gift (Isa. 43:25; Ps. 32:5), so Jesus' pronouncements to some people that their sins were forgiven *here and now* (see Matt. 9:2; Luke 7:48; 18:14) astonished the Jews. He was saying that people could experience this activity of God, which the prophets had promised, *now*.

### Jesus as the Suffering Servant

Christ viewed His entire life and death in the light of the four "Servant" prophecies of Isaiah 42-53* (see Luke 22:37). At His baptism, He heard His Father cite Isaiah's words " 'This is my Son, whom I love; with him I am well pleased' " (Matt. 3:17). From that time on Jesus knew that He had been sent to fulfill the mission of the chosen Servant of Isaiah. Jesus vividly summed up this conviction in His words: " 'The Son of Man did not come to be served, but to serve, and *to give his life as a ransom for many* [*lutron anti pollôn*—literally, "a ransom instead of many"]' " (Mark 10:45, emphasis added). This theme is also the central theme of Isaiah's Servant Songs.

In mentioning "ransom" (*lutron*), Jesus was alluding to the guilt offering of Isaiah 53:10, and His phrase "for many" echoes the re-

---

*Namely, Isaiah 42:1-6; 49:1-6; 50:4-9; and 52:13-53:12

peated "many" in Isaiah 53:11, 12. Jesus even quoted Isaiah 53:12 when He explained the unique purpose of His death: " 'It is written: "And he was numbered with the transgressors"; and I tell you that this must be fulfilled in me. Yes, what is written about me is reaching its fulfillment' " (Luke 22:37).

Jesus' death is of paramount importance for our salvation. It was more than simply the death of a martyr; it accomplished what no other death could. Jesus died an atoning death for the whole world. Many who are lost will be redeemed because He gave His life in their place!*

Jesus gave His life as a guilt offering for others (Isa. 53:10), which makes His death a sacrificial death before God, a death for the forgiveness of sins (see Matt. 26:28). His question " 'Did not the Christ have to suffer these things and then enter his glory?' " (Luke 24:26) reveals that He knew He must suffer on behalf of humankind.

### Jesus' threefold office

Luther and Calvin distinguished three aspects of Jesus' messiahship: His roles as a prophet, as a priest, and as a king. Calvin developed Jesus' threefold office extensively in his *Institutes of the Christian Religion*, stating that we must know His "prophetic office, kingship, and priesthood" to understand the purpose for which the Father sent Jesus.[2]

### Jesus: the greatest Prophet

Jesus' followers recognized Him as a true prophet (Matt. 21:11, 46; Luke 24:19). But Jesus was not merely a prophet who spoke words from God. He was the very embodiment of the Word of God. John called Him "the only begotten God, who is in the bosom of the Father," and he linked this truth about Jesus with Jesus' work of "explaining" the Father (John 1:18, NASB). That Jesus embodied the Word of God marks Him as the greatest prophet.

Moses predicted Jesus' coming as a prophet (see Deut. 18:15, 18, 19); every prophet since Israel's first leader served simply as a type or prophetic foreshadowing of the Messiah. Peter applied Moses'

---

*Jesus used the Greek word *anti*, which means "in the stead of."

ancient prophecy to Jesus in Acts 3:22, 23. And Jesus Himself recognized His prophetic role, announcing it by stating: " 'Now one greater than Jonah is here' " (Matt. 12:41).

As the One sent by the Father, Jesus explained the Scriptures and spoke the words of God with divine authority (Matt. 7:29; John 4:25). Consequently, His words will be the criterion in the last judgment, condemning those who have rejected Him:

"There is a judge for the one who rejects me and does not accept my words; that very word which I spoke will condemn him at the last day. For I did not speak of my own accord, but the Father who sent me commanded me what to say and how to say it" (John 12:48, 49).

Jesus also corrected some erroneous interpretations of the Scriptures and rejected rabbinical additions (Matt. 5:21-37). He not only spoke the truth, He was the "Truth" in person (John 14:6). He asserted without exaggeration: " 'Anyone who has seen me has seen the Father' " (John 14:9).

So, Jesus was indeed the ultimate prophet. He did not claim authority by appealing to Moses, as the rabbis did (Matt. 23:2). He spoke with His own authority, Messianic authority.* He did not look forward to God's kingdom in anticipation, as the prophets had done. Rather, He announced its Messianic fulfillment. "Thus His teaching fulfilled, extended, and clarified that of the [Old Testament] prophetic order. It formed the culmination of their order and the transition to that of the apostles."[3]

## Jesus: the only Mediator

To understand Jesus' work as God's appointed Priest, we must first know the essence of the atoning ministry of the Levitical priests. We can understand Jesus only in the light of the work of these anointed ones of Israel who were appointed to reconcile human beings with the Holy One.

---

*Note, for instance, Jesus' expansions in the Sermon on the Mount: "But I tell you . . ." (Matt. 5:22, 28, 32, 39, 44).

When Scripture lays out the means of reconciliation, it speaks of both an atoning sacrifice and the application of the blood of that sacrifice in the sanctuary of God: "In this way the priest will make atonement for [the repentant sinner], and he will be forgiven" (Lev. 4:26, 31). Likewise, Jesus' fulfillment of His priestly office comprises both His sinless self-sacrifice on our behalf and His continuous intercession for us as the risen Lord.

This priestly work of Jesus constitutes the core of the New Testament witness about Him as the Savior of the world. Jesus' major concern was and is the healing of people from the guilt and the power of sin by His forgiving and restoring grace. When a paralytic was brought before him, Jesus told him: " 'Friend, your sins are forgiven' " (Luke 5:20). According to Leviticus 4:31, only a Levitical priest could make this declaration. The rabbis regarded this hopeless paralytic as under God's curse because of his sins. So, when Jesus pronounced forgiveness, they thought, " 'Who is this fellow who speaks blasphemy? Who can forgive sins but God alone?' " (Luke 5:21).

Jesus read the rabbis' minds and said, " 'Which is easier: to say, "Your sins are forgiven," or to say, "Get up and walk?" But that you may know that the Son of Man has authority on earth to forgive sins . . .' He said to the paralyzed man, ' I tell you, get up, take your mat and go home' " (Luke 5:23, 24). The man's physical healing attested that his soul was restored.

This incident teaches an important lesson for all who suffer from physical disease and who recognize that the burden of sin is the deeper cause of their sickness. Relief comes only from the Healer of the soul. "The peace which He alone can give would impart vigor to the mind, and health to the body."[4] Jesus' marvelous grace and compassion should cause us to be amazed and to praise His name for this assurance of salvation:

O, wondrous love of Christ, stooping to heal the guilty and the afflicted! Divinity sorrowing over and soothing the ills of suffering humanity! Oh, marvelous power thus displayed to the children of men! Who can doubt the message of salvation? Who can slight the mercies of a compassionate Redeemer?[5]

The letter to the Hebrews affirms the abiding power of Jesus' priestly work on the cross and in the heavenly sanctuary. Jesus surpassed the Old Testament types by offering Himself unblemished to God on the cross (Heb. 9:14), becoming thereby "Himself the priest, Himself the victim."[6]

By His resurrection, Jesus immortalized His sacrificial death and gave it an everlasting effectiveness. The redemptive powers of His atoning death work on our behalf each time we celebrate the Lord's Supper and receive the forgiveness of our sins (see Matt. 26:28). But Jesus' priestly work did not end with His resurrection. God ordained Him to sit at His right hand as the supreme King-Priest, in the order of Melchizedek (see Heb. 1:3; 6:20; 7:15, 16). He can now "save completely those who come to God through him, because he always lives to intercede for them" (Heb. 7:25). This means that we may "approach the throne of grace with confidence" and receive from Him mercy and grace "to help us in our time of need" (Heb. 4:16). Our Lord appears now for us in God's presence as our "Advocate" [*Paracletos*], "who speaks to the Father in our defense" (Heb. 9:24; 1 John 2:1).

As a conqueror, Jesus now claims His victory. He absolves those who believe in Him from all charges and frees them from the condemnation of the law of God (see Rom. 8:1, 33, 34). By His Spirit He sustains all who trust in Him so their faith won't fail (Luke 22:32). He has committed Himself to assuring our safe arrival in His kingdom of glory (John 17:24). With such an almighty High Priest presently active (see Rev. 1:12-18), Christians have no further need of human priests, intercessors, or sacrifices.

**Jesus: our eternal King**

The angel Gabriel announced to Mary that her Son would have the name "Jesus" or "Savior" and would be called the Son of the Most High: " 'The Lord God will give him the throne of his father David, and he will reign over the house of Jacob forever; his kingdom will never end' " (Luke 1:31-33). Clearly Jesus was born to fulfill the Messianic promises of the Davidic covenant recorded in 2 Samuel 7:11-13 and Isaiah 9:6, 7; 11:1-5. These prophecies contained the only hope for a lost world.

The so-called Royal Psalms, such as Psalms 2, 45, 89, 110, etc., also make this hope their central theme. These psalms don't express mere pious wishes. Rather, they unfold Nathan's prophecy to David (see 2 Sam. 7) and renew the hope of a coming King-Messiah, whose kingdom of peace and righteousness will last forever.

The New Testament cites and alludes to Psalm 110 thirty-three times, more often than any other psalm—a testimony to this psalm's paramount importance for the gospel witness of the apostolic church. Jesus applied verse one of this psalm to Himself when He said to the high priest, " 'In the future you will see the Son of Man sitting at the right hand of the Mighty One and coming on the clouds of heaven' " (Matt. 26:64). He apparently based His interpretation of this verse on the premise that David had written it. The psalmist ranked two divine persons above himself: Yahweh and his Lord, the Messiah ['*Adoni,* "my Lord"]. Earlier, Jesus' challenge to the Jews had also expressed His conviction: " 'How is it then that David, speaking by the Spirit, calls him [the Christ—the Messiah] "Lord"?' " (Matt. 22:43). These two incidents reveal that Psalm 110 formed a basic pillar of Jesus' understanding of messiahship.

On the day of Pentecost Jesus' apostles received a new understanding of the Messianic fulfillment of this psalm (see Acts 2:34-36). Peter explained the outpouring of the Spirit of God on the apostles as evidence that the crucified and risen Christ was now " 'exalted to the right hand of God' " " 'as Prince and Savior' " (Acts 2:33; 5:31). He explained Jesus' priestly ministry in heaven as that of the predicted Priest-King of Psalm 110:1, 4.

The divine decree of this psalm, " 'Sit at my right hand until I make your enemies a footstool for your feet,' " parallels the divine enthronement of the "Son of Man" in Daniel 7:13, 14—which can be seen as an inspired commentary on Psalm 110.[7] The Messiah receives the highest possible honor: that of sitting next to—not at the feet of—Yahweh to share His authority, power, and glory (cp. Rev. 3:21).

The Messiah shares, even, the authority to judge all humankind (see John 5:22, 27). The Father has placed in the hands of the risen Lord the eternal destinies of all people. Jesus serves at the same time as humanity's Advocate and as its King-Judge. He who knows the weaknesses and temptations sinners face, who poured out His own blood to save them, will deal justly and tenderly with their souls.

Paul stated that God Himself honors His Son because of His self-humiliation and sacrificial love for humankind:

> Therefore God exalted him to the highest place and gave him the name that is above every name, that at the name of Jesus every knee should bow, in heaven and on earth and under the earth, and every tongue confess that Jesus Christ is Lord, to the glory of God the Father (Phil. 2:9-11).

All creatures in the universe will honor, praise, and worship Jesus as the Lord of history and the Savior of mankind, "because you were slain, and with your blood you purchased men for God from every tribe and language and people and nation" (Rev. 5:9).

Shall we not eagerly join this universal choir, singing,

> Worthy, worthy is the Lamb,
> Worthy, worthy is the Lamb;
> Worthy, worthy is the Lamb
> That was slain.
>
> Glory, hallelujah!
> Praise Him, hallelujah!
> Glory, hallelujah
> To the Lamb! —*Anonymous.*

---

1. George Ladd, *A Theology of the New Testament* (Grand Rapids, Mich.: Eerdmans, 1974), 53.

2. *Institutes,* bk. II, ch. 15, heading.

3. W. S. Reid, "Christ; Offices of" *The International Standard Bible Encyclopedia,* rev. ed. (Grand Rapids, Mich.: Eerdmans, 1979), 1:654.

4. E. G. White, *The Desire of Ages,* 270.

5. Ibid., 269, 270.

6. Ibid., 25.

7. According to, for example, E. W. Hengstenberg.

# Chapter 4

# Christ's Assurance
# of Justification

God alone can give us absolute assurance of salvation. Jesus, the Son of God, brought the comforting news that the Father accepts everyone who comes to Jesus and believes in Him. He said:

"All that the Father gives me will come to me, and whoever comes to me I will never drive away. For I have come down from heaven not to do my will but to do the will of him who sent me. And this is the will of him who sent me, that I shall lose none of all that he has given me, but raise them up at the last day. For my Father's will is that everyone who looks to the Son and believes in him shall have eternal life, and I will raise him up at the last day" (John 6:37-40).

God the Father and the Son are perfectly one in their will and acts to save believers from evil and death and even from themselves. The reassuring news is that God has taken the initiative for our redemption. He did not wait till we asked for help. As the Father drew Israel with His everlasting loving kindness (see Jer. 31:3), so He now draws all people and enables them to come to Jesus (see John 6:44, 65). Jesus likewise promised: " 'But I, when I am lifted up from the earth, will draw all men to myself' " (John 12:32). He draws them each time the gospel of the crucified and risen Savior is proclaimed. So, all the glory and honor due those who have provided salvation belong to the divine Father and Son. No one obtains salvation because of personal achievement or merit. From start to finish it is the gift of the gracious God—as Paul said: "The wages of sin is death, but the gift of God is eternal life in Christ Jesus our Lord" (Rom. 6:23).

Ellen G. White emphasized the grace-character of our salvation this way:

> We owe everything to grace, free grace, sovereign grace. Grace in the covenant ordained our adoption. Grace in the Savior effected our redemption, our regeneration, and our adoption to heirship with Christ. Let this grace be revealed to others.[1]

## Salvation as justification by faith

To understand the impact of Jesus' teachings about salvation, we must be aware of what first-century Jews commonly believed about the judgment. The *Testament of Abraham*, an apocryphal Jewish book written between the first and second century, gives us insight into the Judaism of that day. It describes the future judgment scene and the basis on which individuals will receive either life or punishment. E. P. Sanders summed it up:

> If sins not repented of or punished by premature death prior to the judgment outweigh or outnumber righteous deeds, the soul is sentenced to punishment. If righteous deeds predominate, the soul goes to life.[2]

The text states literally: "But if the fire tests the work of anyone and does not touch it, this person is justified and the angel of righteousness takes him and carries him up to the saved in the lot of the righteous."[3] A Jewish scholar affirms: "Judaism had no hesitation about recognizing the merit of good works, or in exhorting men to acquire it and to accumulate a store of merit laid up for the hereafter."[4] In short, even if the credit and debit columns in the account book of heaven are balanced up every day, no Jew could know whether he stands before God justified or condemned.

The story of Rabbi Jochanan ben Zakkai illustrates the plight of those who felt insecure before God. When this old rabbi was dying, he wept continuously. Asked by a disciple why he was weeping, the rabbi replied, "Now when I am being led into the presence of the King of kings, the Holy One, . . . when before me lie two ways, one of Gan Eden and the other of Gehinnom, and *I know not to which I am to be led*—shall I not weep?"[5]

While some Jews felt uncertain about what fate the judgment would decree for them, others confidently believed that their strict law keeping made them righteous before God. Paul, for instance, confessed that as a zealous Pharisee, he felt himself "faultless" regarding legalistic righteousness (see Phil. 3:6). And Jesus addressed the parable of the two worshipers to "some who were confident of their own righteousness and looked down on everybody else" (Luke 18:9). He pointed out that God wouldn't accept the self-righteous prayer of the Pharisee. But of the repentant tax collector who threw himself upon God's mercy, He declared with Messianic authority: " 'I tell you that this man, rather than the other, went home justified before God' " (Luke 18:14). So it was Jesus, and not Paul, who originated the New Testament's doctrine of "righteousness by faith." He equated salvation with forgiveness or justification—an important theological message.

Jesus used this significant parable to teach two concepts new to that time: First, as we have already seen, it is the repentant sinner, not the self-righteous Pharisee, who receives divine justification. And second, justification is not a doubtful event in the future but a divine gift in the present. It is God's present assurance of salvation!

Abram's experience also teaches us truths about justification. Genesis 15:6 says, "Abram believed the LORD, and he credited it to him as righteousness." In Abram's experience, justification was not an antiquated legal concept. Instead, it formed the foundation of a covenant relationship with God, a relationship in which God set the sinner right with Himself. Through sincere repentance the sinner acknowledged what God regards as right and what He considers evil, thereby "justifying" God's judgment (see Ps. 51:4). This was also the essence of the tax collector's confession. He prayed the prayer of King David: " 'God, have mercy on me, a sinner' " (Luke 18:13; see

Ps. 51:1). His attitude revealed true self-knowledge and humility. Jesus commented: " 'Everyone who exalts himself will be humbled, and he who humbles himself will be exalted' " (Luke 18:14). Jesus thus assures divine justification to any repentant sinner at any time, in any culture or society.

People need justification not only at the beginning of the Christian walk but at every step thereafter. Ellen G. White explained this with profound spiritual insight:

> At every advance step in Christian experience our repentance will deepen. . . . We shall make the apostle's confession our own, "I know that in me (that is, in my flesh) dwelleth no good thing" (Rom. 7:18).[6]

Such self-knowledge prevents the believer from falling into the self-sufficiency that characterized Peter when he boasted, " 'Even if all fall away, I will not' " (Mark 14:29). No one is beyond the reach of temptation, as Paul warned, "If you think you are standing firm, be careful that you don't fall!" (1 Cor. 10:12). On the other hand, however, we can enjoy the rest Jesus our Savior offers even now. When He abides in the heart, Jesus brings "a glow of perfect peace, perfect love, perfect assurance."[7]

We must learn to distinguish between a blessed assurance and presumption, a false certainty. Assurance is the fruit of faith and of obedience to God's Word; presumption claims the promises of God in disobedience.

## Justification restores fellowship with God

Jesus regarded justification as more than a purely legal transaction. He considered every act of forgiveness a reclaiming of the sinner for God and His service. He claimed each forgiven sinner as a witness to His Messianic reign over sin and Satan. To a demon-possessed man He said, " 'Go home to your family and tell them how much the Lord has done for you, and how he had mercy on you' " (Mark 5:19). He assured the woman caught in adultery, " 'Neither do I condemn you. . . . Go now and leave your life of sin' " (John 8:11).

He showed a man born blind that He was the creative light of the world, and then He asked him, " 'Do you believe in the Son of Man?' " (John 9:35). He comforted Martha with the words " 'Did I not tell you that if you believed, you would see the glory of God?' " (John 11:40).

Jesus' forgiveness offers every sinner entrance into a transforming fellowship with the Father and Himself. In His Sermon on the Mount Jesus assured His disciples that obtaining salvation means entering God's kingdom and participating in its joy *now*: " '*Blessed are the poor in spirit, for theirs is the kingdom of heaven*' " (Matt. 5:3, emphasis added). It is those who have begun experiencing the deep happiness of the Messianic salvation who are "blessed." Jesus said essentially the same thing when He announced His messiahship in the synagogue: " '*Today* this scripture is fulfilled in your hearing' " (Luke 4:21, emphasis supplied; following His citation of Isaiah 61:1, 2). When the repentant tax collector Zacchaeus declared his conversion and compassion for others, Jesus said, " '*Today* salvation has come to this house.' " (Luke 19:9, emphasis supplied). Jesus expected every redeemed sinner to be grateful for the mercy received and to extend this mercy to others.

Nowhere did Jesus teach the transforming nature of justification more vividly than in His parable of the lost son (see Luke 15:11-32). In this moving story He revealed the restoring power of divine forgiveness and love. The point of the parable is the assurance of the father's abiding love for his wayward son. Ellen G. White commented:

> Miserable as he was, the prodigal found hope in the conviction of his father's love. It was that love which was drawing him toward home. So it is the assurance of God's love that constrains the sinner to return to God. [Rom. 2:4 quoted].[8]

People who doubt the assurance of salvation do so not because some psychological defect prevents them from trusting anyone but because they haven't comprehended the Father's love and compassion for sinners. The prophets emphatically assured Israel of the forgiving love of God. David testified from his own experience: "As a father has compassion on his children, so the LORD has compassion on those who fear him" (Ps. 103:13). Isaiah relayed God's assurances to Israel: " 'I, even I, am he who blots out your transgressions, for my own sake, and remembers your sins no more' " (Isa. 43:25); " 'I have swept away your offenses like a cloud, your sins like the morning mist. Return to me, for I have redeemed you' " (Isa. 44:22). And Micah exalted God's character with these immortal words:

Who is a God like you, who pardons sin and forgives the transgression of the remnant of his inheritance? You do not stay angry forever but delight to show mercy. You will again have compassion on us; you will tread our sins underfoot and hurl all our iniquities into the depth of the sea (Mic. 7:18, 19).

"What assurance here, of God's willingness to receive the re-penting sinner!"[9]

In the parable of the prodigal son, the father does not bring up the sins of his repenting son. "The son feels that the past is forgiven and forgotten, *blotted out forever*."[10] The father embraces him, kisses him, and orders that he be given "the best robe" and that a ring be put on his finger as a sign of reinstatement and sandals on his feet to indicate that he is a free man and not a slave (Luke 15:20, 22). The feast celebrated the father's full acceptance of the prodigal. He was completely and unreservedly restored to the position of son of the master of the estate. That is the full significance of forgiveness, of justification.

### Thankful love as the fruit of assurance

At a feast in the home of Simon the Pharisee in Bethany, Jesus reiterated the important lesson that forgiveness of sins should elicit grateful love. During the meal, Mary, a woman who had been caught up in immorality, had anointed Jesus with costly perfume. She was expressing her profound gratitude for Jesus' message of salvation and for delivering her from evil. Simon did not discern that Mary's desire to give expression to the joy of regeneration motivated her act.

He felt embarrassed by what she had done and began to doubt that Jesus was a prophet.

In that situation Jesus told the parable of two debtors, one of whom owed a small amount and the other a huge amount to the same creditor. When neither could pay back the creditor, he canceled their debts. Jesus challenged Simon, " 'Now which of them will love him more?' " (Luke 7:42). Jesus told the parable to teach us that we ought to appreciate God's forgiving grace and express our appreciation in acts of gratitude.

While Simon showed some appreciation for Jesus' act of healing him from leprosy (Matt. 26:6), Mary's gratitude compelled her to lavish an expensive perfume on her Redeemer. Jesus made this application of His parable: " 'Therefore, I tell you, her many sins have been forgiven—for she loved much. But he who has been forgiven little loves little' " (Luke 7:47). The meaning of the parable is clear. Mary demonstrated great love *because* she had been justified by divine grace, without any work on her part. Jesus reassured this grateful sinner, " 'Your sins are forgiven. . . .Your faith has saved you; go in peace' " (Luke 7:48, 50). Note that it was not her love but her faith in Jesus that had saved her! S. Kistemaker offers this perceptive conclusion:

> We can have the greatest respect for Jesus and can even serve him; but genuine love for him comes only when in Jesus we have experienced remission of sin and assurance of pardon. Then we have learned to know him as Savior; then our love is expressed to him in deeds of gratitude.[11]

**The reward of grace**

Jesus spoke of the sovereign grace and goodness of God in the parable of the vineyard laborers, which might better be called the parable of the gracious employer (Matt. 20:1-16). A question Peter asked occasioned this parable. He said: " 'We have left everything to follow you! What then will there be for us?' " (Matt. 19:27). The Phillips translation reads, " 'What is that going to be worth to us?' " Ellen White explains Peter's motivation as follows: "The disciples were not wholly free from Pharisaism. They still worked with the thought of meriting a reward in proportion to their labor."[12]

To deliver His followers from this mercenary spirit and to illustrate the principles of His kingdom, Jesus told a story. He said a farmer hired several laborers at different hours of the day. He even took on some laborers at the eleventh hour—that is, at 5:00 P.M.; these could work only one hour. The employer arranged a fixed price for the day's labor—one denarius—with the first workers he hired. Those hired later left their wages to his discretion.

In the evening the farmer paid all the laborers the same amount, one denarius. Of course, those who had worked the entire day expected to receive more than what those who had worked only an hour got, and they began to grumble about his justice. The farmer's reply makes the point of the parable: " 'Friend, I am not being unfair to you. Didn't you agree to work for a denarius? . . . *Are you envious because I am generous?'* " (Matt. 20:13, 15, emphasis added). Jesus was saying that human beings are offended by God's grace.

Many Christians do not know the joy of serving the Lord and are motivated instead by a self-caring spirit, a spirit of self-righteousness. That spirit deceives people into thinking they can "do something toward earning a place in the kingdom of heaven."[13] Jesus taught that God's grace cannot be divided into portions. It transcends human justice. The reward that God gives true believers is not something they've merited but a reward of grace, of the undeserved favor of God. "No one is privileged above another, nor can anyone claim the reward as a right."[14] Jesus taught this when He said, " 'You also, when you have done everything you were told to do, should say, "We are unworthy servants; we have only done our duty" ' "(Luke 17:10). The reward for the work we do in God's kingdom depends on God's free pleasure. He won't reward us according to the amount of our labor but according to the riches of His generosity.

The kingdom of God posits the equality of all the redeemed. At the conclusion of His parable Jesus said: " 'So the last will be the first, and the first will be the last' " (Matt. 20:16). He pointed out that the eternal security of the saints doesn't rest on their achievements but on their being children and heirs of God the Father: " 'The King will say to those on his right, "Come, you who are blessed by my Father; take *your inheritance, the kingdom prepared for you since the creation of the world*" ' " (Matt. 25:34).

## God's character: our assurance

God's nature doesn't necessitate His forgiveness of sin, as if that were His job. Nor is forgiveness the suspension of God's justice, as if His justice were severe and harsh. Doubts about our eternal security are rooted in a misconception of God's character—in our failure to grasp the wondrous blend of His justice and mercy, as revealed by God to Moses in Exodus 34:6, 7. It was this harmony of God's attributes that Israel's prophets and psalmists praised, as can be seen in Joel 2:13; Nehemiah 9:31; Jonah 4:2; Psalms 85:10; 86:15; 103:8; 145:8. God intended that the society of His covenant people reflect His divine character by placing justice and mercy on equal terms (see Exod. 22:25-27).

No psalm reflects more accurately the tension repentant believers feel about their standing before God than does Psalm 130. Here the psalmist cries "out of the depths" to the God of Israel. And here he receives assurance:

> If you, O LORD, kept a record of sins, O LORD, who could stand? But with you there is forgiveness; therefore you are feared. . . . O Israel, put your hope in the LORD, for with the LORD is unfailing love and with him is full redemption. He himself will redeem Israel from all their sins (Ps. 130:3, 4, 7, 8).

A troubled conscience can hear no greater assurance than these inspired words of comfort. Many believers have divorced mercy from justice. But in the biblical revelation of God's nature—for example, in Exodus 34:6, 7 and Psalm 85:10—"God's love has been expressed in His justice no less than in His mercy. Justice is the foundation of His throne, and the fruit of His love."[15] This insight does not mean that mercy destroys justice; instead, it means that *both* are the fruits of God's holy love. Such a harmony of God's attributes exceeds all human comprehension! God doesn't bestow His mercy on repentant sinners reluctantly but with delight and with "full redemption" (Isa. 55:7; Ps. 130:7).

Charles H. Spurgeon unfolds this mercy in its great variety:

Here is mercy that receives sinners, mercy that restores back-sliders, mercy that keeps believers. Here is mercy that pardons sin, that introduces to the enjoyment of all gospel privileges, and that blesses the praying soul far beyond its expectations. With the Lord there is mercy, and he loves to display it, he is ready to impart it, he has determined to exalt and to glorify it.[16]

Leslie C. Allen explains the basis of Christian assurance of salvation as follows: "For the Christian this grace is grounded not only in a heart of love but in its disclosure through the death of Jesus as the objective basis of divine deliverance."[17] Jesus demonstrated this holy love and mercy of His Father in His own life and death. He showed that God does not demand justice without mercy, or no one would be saved (see Ps. 143:2). He assured every repentant believer that His self-sacrifice was an all-sufficient ransom for all humankind (Mark 10:45; 1 Tim. 2:6).

---

1. E. G. White, *Testimonies for the Church*, 6:268.

2. *The Old Testament Pseudepigrapha*, J. H. Charlesworth, ed. (Garden City, N.Y.: Doubleday, 1983), 1:878.

3. *Testimony of Abraham*, version A:13:13.

4. G. F. Moore, *Judaism*, 1927, II, 90.

5. *Berakoth* 28b, emphasis added.

6. E. G. White, *Christ's Object Lessons*, 160, 161.

7. Ibid., 420.

8. Ibid., 202.

9. Ibid., 205.

10. Ibid., 204, emphasis added.

11. S. Kistemaker, *The Parables of Jesus* (Grand Rapids, Mich.: Baker Books House, 1980), 164.

12. E. G. White, *Christ's Object Lessons*, 396.

13. Ibid., 400.

14. Ibid., 402.

15. E. G. White, *The Desire of Ages*, 762.

16. Charles H. Spurgeon, *The Treasury of David* (Grand Rapids, Mich.: Zondervan, 1974), 3b:132.

17. *Psalms 101(150*, Word Biblical Commentary (Waco, Tex.: Word Books, 1983), 21:196.

# Chapter 5

# Paul's Assurance
# of Salvation

Paul formulated his gospel message from the perspective of his own experience of salvation and background as a Pharisee. Three times he described his dramatic conversion from Saul the persecutor to Paul the disciple (Acts 9; 22; 26). This witness remains one of the main pillars on which Christianity is founded. It is highly significant that the zealous Pharisee and member of the Sanhedrin, who went all the way to Damascus to apprehend and prosecute Jewish Christians, did not become a Christian merely by meditating on the Old Testament or by desperately accumulating work-righteousness. Instead, his Christianity arose from a personal encounter with the risen Lord Jesus. He saw the Crucified One as a glorious Being and heard His voice asking him personally: " 'Saul! Saul! Why do you persecute me?' " When he asked, " 'Who are you, Lord?' " the answer was: " 'I am Jesus of Nazareth' " (Acts 22:7, 8).

This encounter led Saul of Tarsus to rethink his Pharisaic theology and piety. The overwhelming reality of the resurrection of Jesus as the divine Messiah gave Saul a different perspective on the Messianic prophecies. "No doubt entered the mind of Saul that the One who spoke to him was Jesus of Nazareth, the long-looked-for Messiah, the Consolation and Redeemer of Israel."[1] It wasn't the testimony of the apostles that convinced him of the gospel's truth: "I did not receive it from any man, nor was I taught it; rather, I received it by revelation from Jesus Christ" (Gal. 1:12). The historic encounter with the risen Lord gave Paul the unassailable assurance of both his salvation and his calling as an apostle of Christ Jesus. All doubt disappeared in that moment of divine revelation—as Ellen White commented:

> Now that Jesus Himself stood revealed, Saul was convinced of the truthfulness of the claims made by the disciples. . . . Now Saul knew for a certainty that the promised Messiah had come to this earth as Jesus of Nazareth.[2]

## Paul's transforming gospel

Paul's religious education undoubtedly influenced the particular burden of his apostolic letters. The fundamental change of his theology encouraged him to contrast salvation by grace through faith in Jesus with salvation by works of law. (His concept of "law" included the moral law of God as well, as is generally recognized.) The change from a law-centered theology and piety to a Christ-centered way of salvation and lifestyle comprised the essence of his radical conversion. He realized that to seek merit before God was to misunderstand the message of Israel's prophets and to misread the far-reaching claims of God's law. His rejection of a law-centered theology and piety didn't mean a denigration of God's law, however. He recognized that Jesus had come "for the express purpose of vindicating His Father's law."[3] He saw that the rabbinic understanding of the old covenant was unenlightened and even obstructed the insight disclosed by Israel's Messiah.

Paul compared the stifled condition of his contemporary Jews with that of the Israelites who asked Moses to don a veil to shield them from the glory of God that shone from his face (2 Cor. 3:13; Exod. 34:33). Paul interpreted this spirit of self-preservation as a dullness of mind that still existed in his day:

> Their minds were made dull, for to this day the same veil remains when the old covenant is read. It has not been removed, because only in Christ is it taken away. Even to this day when Moses is read, a veil covers their hearts. But whenever anyone turns to the Lord, the veil is taken away (2 Cor. 3:14-16).

Paul went on to say that reading the Scriptures in the light of the rabbinic tradition, later codified in the Talmud, gives but a dim view of the Messianic deliverance from all works-righteousness and self-justification. His former legalistic understanding of salvation could not compare with the transforming joy and freedom of Christ Jesus. He testified of this difference as follows:

> We, who with unveiled faces all reflect the Lord's glory, are being transformed into his likeness with ever increasing glory, which comes from the Lord, who is the Spirit (2 Cor. 3:18).

Paul now knew the joy of salvation and of a growing fellowship with the risen Lord through the Holy Spirit. And he didn't limit such freedom and joy to himself but said that *all* Christian believers experience God's glory in this way (see verse 18). This passage conveys Paul's gospel of assurance, a gospel that provides an ever-increasing growth in the knowledge and grace of Christ.

The light Christians receive, the light that shines from Jesus, enlightens the mind and revives the soul. Paul even compared the power of the gospel to God's act of creation in the beginning: "For God, who said, 'Let light shine out of the darkness,' made his light shine in our hearts to give us the light of the knowledge of the glory of God in the face of Christ" (2 Cor. 4:6). If God Himself acts in the proclamation of the gospel of Christ, then the persistent rejection of that gospel issues from a supernatural, demonic blinding: "The god of this age has blinded the minds of unbelievers, so that they cannot see the light of the gospel of the glory of Christ, who is the image of God" (2 Cor. 4:4).

### Paul's polemical statements

To clarify the fundamental contrast between salvation by law observance and salvation by the grace of God in Jesus, Paul emphasized that the believer is justified by grace *without* any law observance:

> Through him [Jesus] everyone who believes is justified from everything you could not be justified from by the law of

Moses (Acts 13:39).

No one will be declared righteous in his sight by observing the law; rather, through the law we become conscious of sin. But now a righteousness from God, apart from law, has been made known, to which the Law and the Prophets testify. . . . For we maintain that a man is justified by faith apart from observing the law (Rom. 3:20, 21, 28).

We who are Jews by birth and not Gentile sinners know that a man is not justified by observing the law, but by faith in Jesus Christ. So we, too, have put our faith in Christ Jesus that we may be justified by faith in Christ and not by observing the law, because by observing the law no one will be justified (Gal. 2:15, 16).

I do not set aside the grace of God, for if righteousness could be gained through the law, Christ died for nothing! (Gal. 2:21).

Clearly no one is justified before God by the law, because, "The righteous will live by faith" (Gal. 3:11).

It is by grace you have been saved, through faith—and this not from yourselves, it is the gift from God—not by works, so that no one can boast (Eph. 2:8, 9).

Paul appealed to Moses, the Psalms, and the Prophets, citing passages that deserve our careful attention: Genesis 15:6; Psalm 143:2; Habakkuk 2:4. A close comparison of the way Paul used these three Old Testament texts reveals that he constantly added a personal note that stresses the antithesis of grace and works more sharply: "Apart from law" (Rom. 3:21); "apart from observing the law" (Rom. 3:28); "not by works, so that no one can boast" (Eph. 2:9).

This radical contrast of two concepts of salvation directly affects our assurance of God's acceptance: Our salvation is based on the grace of God alone! His choice and electing love secure our salvation. Paul never got tired of stressing: "If by grace, then it is no longer by works; if it were, grace would no longer be grace" (Rom. 11:6). He defined "works of the law" as merit-seeking works and placed all who "are of the works of the law under a curse" (Gal. 3:10, NASB). Other versions translate: "All who rely on observing the law are under a curse" (NIV) or "All who rely on the works of the law are under a curse" (NRSV).

Paul didn't consider the law itself a curse. Far from it! He characterized the law as "holy, righteous and good" (Rom. 7:12; see also Gal. 3:21). No, he wanted to clarify two mutually exclusive concepts of justification, two ways of salvation: righteousness *either* by law-observance *or* by Christ. He summed this up in these words: "I do not set aside the grace of God, for if righteousness could be gained through the law, Christ died for nothing!" (Gal. 2:21). So, Paul did not contrast law with grace; instead, he contrasted attempts to attain righteousness or justification through observance of the law with God's gracious provision of those qualities.

Paul strongly denied that there are two paths to salvation. One can find justification before God only through faith in Jesus—that is, by God's gift of Jesus' righteousness imputed to the repentant sinner: "This righteousness from God comes through faith in Jesus Christ to all who believe" (Rom. 3:22). This good news transformed Paul's entire theology and piety, and later that of Luther. It still liberates the thinking and believing of many Christians who used to look to their efforts to make them acceptable to God.

The following autobiographic passage is of paramount importance for understanding Paul's emphasis on justification as the only assurance of our eternal salvation. He wrote to the saints at Philippi that he no longer trusted in his virtues or sought his security in the merits of his achievements:

Whatever was to my profit I now consider loss for the sake of Christ. What is more, I consider everything a loss compared to the surpassing greatness of knowing Christ Jesus my Lord, for whose sake I have lost all things. I consider them rubbish, that I may gain Christ and be found in him, not having a righteousness of my own that comes from the law, but that which is through faith in Christ—the righteousness that comes from God and is by faith (Phil. 3:7-9).

Paul illustrated this saving truth with two historical examples from the Old Testament: Abram and David (see Rom. 4:1-8). These two Hebrew believers received the divine gift of justification by faith alone (see Gen. 15:6; Ps. 32:1, 2). Paul appealed to these texts to establish the essential continuity of Christian and Hebrew faith. There is only *one* way of salvation.

## Sanctification by faith in Jesus

Because of Paul's emphasis on justification "apart from law," he was accused of teaching a gospel of lawlessness (see Rom. 3:8; 6:1, 15). His opponents claimed that his message that the wicked were "justified in Christ" merely promoted more sinning (Rom. 4:5; Gal. 2:17). Such an objection could rise only if one assumed that Paul taught a compartmentalized, purely forensic (legal) doctrine of justification. But Paul's reply in Galatians 2:17-20 shows that such an interpretation of his gospel is a fundamental misunderstanding: "Absolutely not!" he said (v. 17).

Paul refuted the false charge by explaining that faith in Jesus means a *transforming* union of the soul with Jesus: "I have been cru-cified with Christ and I do no longer live, but Christ lives within me. The life I live in the body, I live by faith in the Son of God, who loved me and gave himself for me" (Gal. 2:20). So Paul answered the charge of antinomianism by pointing to *the transforming power of the in-dwelling Christ* (see also Eph. 3:17). This means that God doesn't merely impute or reckon His righteousness to the repentant sinner, He also imparts it. His righteousness enters into the soul and life of the forgiven believer. Paul said: "The only thing that counts is faith expressing itself through love" (Gal. 5:6). This establishes an organic or living connection between justification and sanctification, the ethi-cal dynamic between faith and love in those who are "in Christ."

Paul developed this relationship in Romans 5-8. He first ex-plained that justification by faith evidences its presence through cer-tain fruits: peace of conscience with God, fellowship with God, and joy in the hope of sharing the glory of God (see Rom. 5:1, 2). Then he pointed to the new power in the life of the believer: the Holy Spirit has entered the heart with the love of God and the personal assurance of life eternal (Rom. 5:5). Paul stated: *"The Spirit himself testifies with our spirit that we are God's children. Now if we are children, then we are heirs—heirs of God and co-heirs with Christ,* if indeed we share in his sufferings in order that we may also share in his glory" (Rom. 8:16, 17, emphasis added). Each believer in Jesus has received a unique assurance from the Spirit of God that he or she is a child of the Father in heaven and therefore has a right to God's eternal glory! This assurance does not rest on our sanctified life or on any of our virtues but exclusively on God's gift of justification in Jesus. God expects in return not an argument but gratitude and worship that praises His everlasting mercy.

Paul reassures us once again that because of our justification

> *there is now no condemnation for those who are in Christ Jesus,* because through Christ Jesus the law of the Spirit of life set me free from the law of sin and death. . . . Who will bring any charge against those whom God has chosen? *It is God who justifies. Who is he that condemns? Christ Jesus,* who died—more than that, who was raised to life—is at the right hand of God and *is also interceding for us* (Rom. 8:1, 33, 34, emphasis added).

Paul's theology of assurance rests on this cornerstone: that believers are justified by faith in Christ because they are "in Christ" and placed under His reign and priestly dominion (see Col. 1:13). This comforting message is an essential part of the apostolic gospel.

Justification functions as more than merely the first step of our Christian walk. We need it daily for our new life in Jesus. His heavenly mediation is essential because of believers' constant commission of sin. At the end of the first century John wrote: "My dear children, I write this to you so that you will not sin. But if anybody does sin, we have one who speaks to the Father in our defense—Jesus Christ, the Righteous One. He is the atoning sacrifice for our sins, and not only for ours but also for the sins of the whole world" (1 John 2:1, 2).

John warned believers not to "claim to be without sin" because then they would deceive themselves (1 John 1:8). Since all our worship passes "through the corrupt channels of humanity" and is therefore defiled, even our prayers and praise are acceptable to God only through the cleansing blood of Jesus. Ellen White exclaimed: "Oh, that all may see that everything in obedience, in penitence, in praise and thanksgiving, must be placed upon the glowing fire of the righteousness of Christ."[4] Our assurance of salvation does not rest on our efforts to obey the law of God perfectly nor on our living holy and unselfish lives. While we may enjoy the favor of God and claim to obey His commandments, "we are not to be anxious about what Christ and God think of us, but about what God thinks of Christ, our Substitute. Ye are accepted in the Beloved."[5]

Our absolute certainty of eternal life is anchored in God's election of Jesus as our Representative and Substitute: "In him we were also chosen, having been predestined according to the plan of him who works out everything in conformity with the purpose of his will" (Eph. 1:11). Paul explained that whoever believes the gospel of Christ is "marked in him [Christ] with a seal, the promised Holy Spirit, *who is a deposit guaranteeing our inheritance* until the redemption of those who are God's possession—to the praise of his glory" (Eph. 1:13, 14, emphasis added; see also 2 Cor. 5:5).

So, the present gift of the Spirit, even in His fullness, is still only a small portion of what God has planned for us to receive—a divine pledge or earnest of the coming glory. Paul unfolded this more in the following consolation: "We ourselves, who have the firstfruits of the Spirit, groan inwardly as we wait eagerly for our adoption as sons, the redemption of our bodies. For in this hope we are saved" (Rom. 8:23, 24). Christian assurance thus includes both our present and our future salvation. The gift of the Holy Spirit is the divine seal in the heart "for the day of redemption" in glory (Eph. 4:30).

One cannot retain justification without a sanctified life, because Jesus cannot be divided. To have received Jesus means to have received justification, sanctification, and glorification (see 1 Cor. 1:30; Rom. 8:29, 30). Nevertheless, justification is the root, and sanctification and glorification are the fruits. Ellen White portrayed the connection this way: "The righteousness by which we are justified is imputed; the righteousness by which we are sanctified is imparted. The first is our title to heaven, the second is our fitness for heaven."[6]

## The most comprehensive vision of salvation

A vision of the prophet Zechariah offers what is perhaps the most vivid illustration of the process of salvation. The people of Judah had just returned from the Babylonian captivity. Zechariah sees the high priest, Joshua, who represented God's people in the temple services, standing before the angel of God. Satan stands to Joshua's right to bring accusations against him—representing his accusations against God's people.

God's reply to Satan's accusations is of profound significance: The LORD has "chosen Jerusalem"! (Zech. 3:2). This divine election generates Israel's acceptance and high calling before God. Israel had sinned; the vision depicted the high priest "dressed in filthy clothes" (v. 3; see Mal. 2:11-17). But in His mercy God commanded: "Take off his filthy clothes" (v. 4). The rest of the verse clarifies the meaning of this order: "See, I have taken away your sin, and I will put rich garments [festal robes, NASB] on you" (v. 4).

What a comforting assurance! This act of divine justification is a *double* transaction: taking off the dirty clothes and putting on clean ones. It portrays the full meaning of divine forgiveness. That forgiveness provides more than just pardon or amnesty; it includes God's gracious restoration to a righteous standing before Him. This is the essence of God's amazing grace, made more sure by Jesus' atoning death. Ellen White explained God's forgiving grace with these assuring words of Jesus: "I will blot out his transgressions. I will cover his sins. I will impute to him My righteousness."[7] So, Zechariah compares the forgiven sinner to a "burning stick snatched from the fire" (Zech. 3:2). The "clean turban" placed on the head of the high priest signifies the seal of approval that reinstates him to serve God as priest.

In Zechariah's vision the restored high priest is called to obey and serve his Redeemer: "This is what the LORD Almighty says: 'If you will walk in my ways and keep my requirements, then you will govern my house and have charge of my courts, and I will give you a place among these standing here' " (Zech. 3:7). Justification, then,

obliges to sanctification—and receives the wonderful promise of glorification.

So, today, all the followers of Jesus who have sinned but who
have not surrendered themselves to the control of evil and are willing
to serve their Redeemer with an everlasting gratitude may apply
Zechariah's vision to themselves. "All that have put on the robe of
Christ's righteousness will stand before Him as chosen and faithful
and true. Satan has no power to pluck them out of the hand of Christ."[8]
Such can find renewed comfort and assurance in these words of promise:

> Grace is an attribute of God exercised toward undeserving
> human beings. We did not seek for it, but it was sent in search
> of us. God rejoices to bestow His grace upon us, not because
> we are worthy, but because we are so utterly unworthy. Our
> only claim to His mercy is our great need.[9]

What a gracious privilege! What a glorious hope!

---

1. E. G. White, *The Acts of the Apostles*, 117.

2. Ibid., 115, 116.

3. Ibid., 120.

4. E. G. White, *Selected Messages*, 1:344.

5. Ibid., 2:32, 33.

6. E. G. White, *Review and Herald*, 4 June 1895; quoted in *Messages to Young People*,
35.

7. E. G. White, MS 125, 1901; quoted in *SDA Bible Commentary*, 4:1178, on Zech.
3:4, 5.

8. E. G. White, *Testimonies for the Church*, 5:471.

9. E. G. White, *Ministry of Healing*, 161.

## Chapter 6

# Peter's Experience of Salvation

The story of Simon Peter's life, his spontaneity and courage in spite of his shortcomings and failures, has been an enduring inspiration to all who identify with him. It shows how Christians can change at heart and grow in faith, love, and hope. Jesus saw great value in Peter's zealous and uncompromising character. When converted, Peter became one of the best-loved apostles because of his passionate loyalty and devotion. His life testifies to the transforming power of God's grace.

Andrew, Peter's brother, was a follower of John the Baptist. One day he saw John pointing to Jesus and heard him say: " 'Look, the Lamb of God!' " (John 1:36). Andrew found Peter, told him " 'We have found the Messiah!' " and led him to Jesus (John 1:41, 42). When Jesus saw Peter, He said: " 'You are Simon son of John. You will be called Cephas' "—or "Peter," meaning "rolling stone" (John 1:42).

Both Andrew and Peter became followers of Jesus. They accepted Jesus as the Messiah in His state of humiliation, before He was crowned the Lord of glory—though this does not imply that they understood His mission, His suffering and death on a cross.

When Jesus neared the end of His ministry on earth, He wanted to prepare His disciples for the trials they would face. In Caesarea Philippi He asked them " 'Who do you say I am?' " Peter immediately replied, " 'You are the Christ, the Son of the living God' " (Matt. 16:16). Peter's confession of faith is the foundational creed of all true believers. It declares what qualifies people to receive life eternal (see John 17:3). Neither human wisdom nor goodness produces this faith. Jesus pointed to God Himself as its source: " 'Blessed are you, Simon son of Jonah, for this was not revealed to you by man, but by my Father in heaven' " (Matt. 16:17). In other words, God gives faith in Jesus as the Messiah of prophecy as a gracious gift; it doesn't come as the result of human reasoning.

Jesus certified Peter's confession of faith as true and approved by divine authority. He honored Peter as the representative of the other apostles and of all true believers and entrusted him with the "keys of the kingdom of heaven" (Matt. 16:19). These "keys" do not symbolize authority over other believers. Rather, they represent the authoritative teaching that opens the door to life eternal. The key was given originally to Israel's priests and teachers (Mal. 2:7). But Jesus perceived a persistent misuse of their high calling, and so He rebuked the rabbis of His time: " 'Woe to you experts in the law, because *you have taken away the key to knowledge.* You yourselves have not entered, and you have hindered those who were entering' " (Luke 11:52, emphasis added); " 'You shut the kingdom of heaven in men's faces' " (Matt. 23:13).

Ellen White explained this passage in terms of the testimony of Jesus:

> "The keys of the kingdom of heaven" are the words of Christ. All the words of Holy Scripture are His, and are here included. These words have power to open and to shut heaven. They declare the conditions upon which men are received or rejected.[1]

So, Peter and the other apostles (Matt. 18:18) could now open the door to salvation. And people were to understand that this door did not open on the basis of obedience to the Torah but rather on the basis of the gospel proclamation of Jesus (see Matt. 10:13-15). We may even conclude that God gave the power of the keys to all the witnesses of Jesus as a whole.

The following words of Jesus, which are the most controversial in all of Scripture, are highly significant:

"And I tell you that you are Peter, and on this rock I will build my church, and the gates of Hades will not overcome it" (Matt. 16:18).

The metaphorical use of "build" indicates that Jesus was comparing His church with a spiritual house or temple. He is building His church on an immovable "rock," which the prophet Isaiah referred to as the foundation stone: " 'See, I lay a stone in Zion, a tested stone, a precious cornerstone for a sure foundation; the one who trusts will never be dismayed' " (Isa. 28:16). Peter cited this text, applying it to Jesus as "the living Stone" on which all believers are built "like living stones" into "a spiritual house to be a holy priesthood" (1 Pet. 2:4-6). So, neither Peter nor the apostles but Jesus Himself as the Messiah of prophecy is the rock on which He builds the church. Peter and the apostles can fulfill their calling as apostles only because Jesus is the God-appointed Christ.

This gospel message opens and closes the door to salvation (see 1 Pet. 2:7, 8). In this sense we can also say that Jesus builds His church on the truth that Peter confessed. Together with the other apostles, Peter was a founding father of the church of which Jesus is the unique bedrock (see Eph. 2:19-22; 1 Cor. 3:11). Nothing can ever destroy this church. On the day of Pentecost, the Spirit-filled Peter exclaimed: " 'Salvation is found in no one else, for there is no other name under heaven given to men by which we must be saved' " (Acts 4:12). Peter maintained this confession of faith till the end of his life.

## Peter's growth in the grace of Christ

Accepting Jesus as the Christ does not imply that one understands the mission of the Messiah. When Peter became a disciple, he still believed that Jesus would reign on earth as a temporal prince. That's why he objected to Jesus' revelation that He had to suffer and "must be killed." " 'Never, Lord!' " Peter objected. " 'This shall never happen to you!' " (Matt. 16:21, 22).

The temptation to avoid the cross was the strongest temptation Jesus had to face. Earlier, in the wilderness, Satan had posed this temptation to Jesus (Matt. 4:8, 9). Now Peter advanced the same temptation, which reminded Jesus of Satan's effort. Jesus immediately replied: " 'Get behind me, Satan! You are a stumbling block to me; you do not have in mind the things of God, but the things of men' " (Matt. 16:23). His reaction shows how essential His atoning death was to His mission.

Peter had to learn Jesus' mission through a bitter experience, an experience that transformed him into a humble follower of Jesus in suffering and death. Near the end of His ministry, after the Last Supper, Jesus announced that all of His disciples would desert Him. Peter spontaneously exclaimed, " 'Even if all fall away on account of you, I never will' " (Matt. 26:33). But then Jesus was arrested and brought before the authorities, and Peter began to fear what might happen to him if he acknowledged his relationship to Jesus. So that very night he disowned his Master three times, swearing with an oath that he didn't even know Him (Matt. 26:69-74).

Jesus didn't reject Peter because of his shameful denials. Instead, Jesus accepted Peter's sincere, heart-rending repentance. When He appeared to His apostles after His resurrection, He asked Peter specifically three times whether he really loved Him. And three times Peter answered that he did love Him. Each time, then, Jesus entrusted Peter with pastoral responsibility for the church, thereby reestablishing him as a trustworthy apostle: " 'Feed my lambs' "; " 'Take care of my sheep' "; " 'Feed my sheep' " (John 21:15-17).

> Three times Peter had openly denied his Lord, and three times Jesus drew from him the assurance of his love and loyalty, pressing home that pointed question, like a barbed arrow to his wounded heart. Before the assembled disciples Jesus revealed the depth of Peter's repentance, and showed how thoroughly humbled was the once boasting disciple.[2]

Jesus had prayed for Peter that his faith might not fail, stating " 'when you have turned back, strengthen your brothers' " (Luke 22:32). Peter always remembered the threat his bravado and spiritual self-dependence posed. Jesus' acceptance of the repenting disciple transformed him into a caring shepherd who had the essential qualification of discipleship and service: love for Jesus. Now he was willing to suffer and to die on a cross for his Lord (see John 21:18, 19). And "when at last brought to the cross, he was, at his own request, crucified with his head downward. He thought it too great an honor to suffer in the same way as his Master did."[3]

## Peter's growing understanding of God's plan

After his recommissioning, Peter focused all his witnessing on his countrymen, the Jews. But in Joppa God gave him a vision that broke through the cultural tradition of Judaism and enlarged his restricted view of God's saving grace. God called Peter to go to a Roman centurion named Cornelius who lived in Caesarea and who led his family in the worship of the God of Israel.

One day while Cornelius was praying, an angel came to him and said: " 'Your prayers and gifts to the poor have come up as a memorial offering before God. Now send men to Joppa to bring back a man named Simon who is called Peter' " (Acts 10:4, 5). The angel's instruction teaches us an important lesson. It tells us that God wants human beings, not angels, to proclaim the gospel in the world. Ellen G. White clarifies: "It is the plan of Heaven that those who have received light shall impart it to those in darkness."[4]

Soon thereafter, Peter received a vision during his prayer on the rooftop of his lodging. Three times he saw a large sheet that contained all kinds of unclean animals lowered from heaven. A voice told him to kill and eat them. When he refused in obedience to the law of Moses, the voice said, " 'Do not call anything impure that God has made clean' " (Acts 10:9-16). Immediately after this vision, three men Cornelius had sent arrived at the house where Peter was staying and asked that he return with them to Caesarea and share his gospel with the centurion.

In Caesarea, Peter found a large crowd waiting to hear what he had to say. Then he understood the meaning of his own vision: " 'God has shown me that I should not call any man impure or unclean' " (Acts 10:28). He realized that God's election of Israel was not God's selecting a favorite; rather, it was His commissioning a nation to witness to all people (see Acts 10:34-43). Peter then preached

Jesus as the sinner's only hope. And when—to his amazement and that of the other Jews—the Holy Spirit descended on the believing Gentiles, Peter "ordered them baptized in the name of Jesus Christ" (Acts 10:48).

Ellen White described the significance of Peter's vision:

> It revealed to him the purpose of God—that by the death of Christ the Gentiles should be made fellowheirs with the Jews to the blessings of salvation. As yet none of the disciples had preached the gospel to the Gentiles. In their minds the middle wall of partition, broken down by the death of Christ, still existed, and their labors had been confined to the Jews, for they had looked upon the Gentiles as excluded from the blessings of the gospel. Now the Lord was seeking to teach Peter the world-wide extent of the divine plan.[5]

The Jewish Christians in Jerusalem challenged what Peter had done. But when he gave an account of his actions, they praised God for the divine initiative: " 'So then, God has granted even the Gentiles repentance unto life' " (Acts 11:18). Thus God used Peter in a mighty way to expand the church's missionary work, opening their vision to the Gentile world.

That didn't mean, however, that Peter became an unfailing beacon of light. In Antioch of Syria, a Christian center, Paul rebuked Peter for failing to represent the principle of the equality of the Gentiles with the Jews. Paul stated, "I opposed him to his face, because he was clearly in the wrong [literally, "because he stood condemned," NASB]" (Gal. 2:11). Paul tells why Peter stood condemned before God: At the arrival of a delegation from the Jerusalem church, Peter had withdrawn from table fellowship with Gentile believers "because he was afraid of those who belonged to the circumcision group" (Gal. 2:12). Peter injudiciously separated himself from the Gentile Christians in order to appease the conservative Jewish Christians, who believed that all Gentile believers must observe the cultic and dietary laws of Moses.

Such conduct by a "pillar" of the church (see Gal. 2:9) had "serious implications for the proclamation of the gospel to Gentiles and for a doctrine of the oneness of the body of Christ."[6] It threatened the church with division. Paul perceived the subverting influence of Peter's doublehearted example and "openly rebuked him for thus disguising his true sentiments."[7] He saw this act as a betrayal of the truth of the gospel, because it would force Gentile believers to follow Jewish customs (see Gal. 2:14).

Ellen White commented on this episode: "This record of the apostle's weakness was to remain as a proof of his fallibility and of the fact that he stood in no way above the level of the other apostles."[8] But "Peter saw the error into which he had fallen, and immediately set about repairing the evil that had been wrought, so far as was in his power."[9] Thus Peter showed a willingness to admit his failure and to respect the counsel of his fellow apostle Paul and the authority of the general council of Jerusalem (see Acts 15:19, 20, 28, 29).

### Peter's theology of hope

Peter's two apostolic letters show that he was a theologian in his own right. He considered himself one of "God's elect" who was a "stranger" in the world (1 Pet. 1:1). He called himself a "fellow elder" and thus did not claim a higher office than the elders in the local churches (1 Pet. 5:1). According to a tradition found in the apocryphal *Acts of Peter*, he was crucified outside Rome in the last years of Emperor Nero. Peter's letters were therefore written probably about the years 63-64.

Peter wrote his first letter to inspire the suffering Christians of Asia Minor with new hope and to encourage them to persevere in their trials. He made the word *hope* a key word in his first letter (see 1 Pet. 1:3, 21; 3:5, 15). "He wants the believers to understand that when they suffer, they are not undergoing a futile exercise but are submitting themselves to a divine test designed to prove their faith (1:7)."[10]

Peter grounded the Christian hope on the written Word of God and on its promises of an imperishable inheritance and an earth made new (see 1 Pet. 1:4; 2 Pet. 3:13). Even now, through the experience of rebirth and new love, the believer shares in this promise: "For you have been born again, not of perishable seed, but of imperishable, through the living and enduring word of God [Isa. 40:6-8 quoted]" (1 Pet. 1:23-24). By the "living and enduring word of God," Peter meant the transforming power of the gospel (1 Pet. 1:25). Humankind's present experience of salvation guarantees their future glory. Believers who have "tasted that the Lord is good" have the privilege and duty to grow up in their salvation by obeying the truth and expressing love to others (1 Pet. 1:22; 2:2, 3).

Peter pointed out:

[God's] divine power has given us everything we need for life and godliness through our knowledge of him who called us by his own glory and goodness. Through these he has given us his very great and precious promises, so that through them you may participate in the divine nature and escape the corruption in the world caused by evil desires (2 Pet.1:3, 4).

In the subsequent verses (5-7) Peter indicated the need for constant growth in the grace and knowledge of Christ, describing a spiritual "ladder" of sanctification. To climb this ladder means "to make your calling and election sure" (2 Pet. 1:10). He explained: "For if you do these things, you will never fall, and you will receive a rich welcome into the eternal kingdom of our Lord and Savior Jesus Christ" (2 Pet. 1:10, 11). Peter had learned the lesson himself after his earlier mistakes. Jesus' grace transformed him into a courageous witness and a moral example for all believers. He climbed round after round on the ladder of Christian progress: faith, goodness, knowledge, self-control, perseverance, godliness, brotherly kindness, love. What a wonderful calling and privilege!

Ellen White has commented: "We are saved by climbing round after round, mounting step after step, to the height of Christ's ideal for us. Thus He is made unto us wisdom, and righteousness, and sanctification, and redemption."[11] Peter did not consider a sanctified life an option for Christians; it is, rather, our constant high calling and election. He regarded a neglect to follow Jesus as being spiritually "nearsighted and blind," and as forgetting that we have "been cleansed from [our] past sins" (2 Pet. 1:9).

Peter emphasized that the church of Christ is the essential continuation of spiritual Israel, with the same election and calling: to "declare the praises of him who called you out of darkness into his wonderful light" (1 Pet. 2:9). The descriptive terms he applied to the church—"a royal priesthood, a holy nation, a people belonging to God" (v. 9)—renew God's instruction to Israel at Mount Sinai: " 'You will be for me a kingdom of priests and a holy nation' " (Exod. 19:6; also see Deut. 7:6). From the beginning to the end of his first epistle, Peter designated both Jesus and the church as *chosen* by God (1 Pet. 1:2; 2:4, 6, 9; 5:13). He closed this letter with the significant statement that church members are "in Christ" (1 Pet. 5:14).

While Peter had been an eyewitness of Jesus' glorification on the mount and had heard the voice of the Father say " 'This is my Son, whom I love. . . . Listen to him!' " (Matt. 17:5), he still based his certainty of faith and hope on the sacred Scriptures: "We have the word of the prophets made more certain, and you will do well to pay attention to it, as to a light shining in a dark place, until the day dawns and the morning star rises in your hearts" (2 Pet. 1:19; also see 3:13).

Shortly before the aged apostle was called to martyrdom for his faith, he once more drew attention to the privilege of every believer. His words challenge us yet today: "Grow in the grace and knowledge of our Lord and Savior Jesus Christ. To him be glory both now and forever! Amen" (2 Pet. 3:18).

---

1. E. G. White, *The Desire of Ages*, 414.

2. Ibid., 812.

3. Ibid., 816.

4. E. G. White, *The Acts of the Apostles*, 134.

5. Ibid., 135, 136.

6. R. N. Longenecker, *Galatians*, Word Biblical Commentary (Dallas: Word Books, 1990), 41:75.

7. E. G. White, *The Acts of the Apostles*, 198.

8. Ibid., 198, 199.

9. Ibid., 198.

10. S. J. Kistemaker, *Peter and Jude* (Grand Rapids, Mich.: Baker Book House, 1987), 21.

11. E. G. White, *The Acts of the Apostles*, 530.

## Chapter 7

# John's Assurance of Salvation

John's experience of God's transforming grace makes a unique contribution to our understanding of the assurance of salvation. John pointed to the self-sacrificing love of God the Father as the basis of our eternal security (see John 3:16). He stated his message briefly: "This is the testimony: God has given us eternal life, and this life is in his Son" (1 John 5:11). John's entire Gospel emphasizes that Jesus is the eternal Son of the Father, sent into the world for humanity's salvation.

John emphasized the essential unity of the Father and the Son in Their will to draw *all* people to Themselves and into Their divine fellowship of love. This means that Jesus, the Son of God, secures our assurance of salvation, which becomes effectual through personal surrender—through yielding to Jesus' call. Even the prospect of the final judgment cannot threaten such a certainty of faith and salvation as long as our faith remains centered on Jesus. In fact, John viewed the personal decision of faith as a judgment by which the believer is transferred from death to life and begins to participate in the powers of the coming age (John 5:24). He stated in clear terms why he wrote his Gospel: "These [stories of Jesus' miraculous signs] are written that you may believe that Jesus is the Christ [Messiah], the Son of God, and that by believing you may have life in his name" (John 20:31). John's words imply that saving faith involves both believing *in* Jesus and believing *that* He is the Christ, the Son of God.

D. A. Carson clarified this point:

John's presentation of *who Jesus is* lies at the heart of all that is distinctive in this Gospel. . . . To hammer away at the urgency of belief without pausing to think through *what* it is John wants his readers to believe and *whom* it is he wants them to trust is to betray the Gospel of John.[1]

John taught that the assurance of life eternal comes through knowing Jesus as the Son of God and divine Messiah: " 'Now this is eternal life: that they may know you, the only true God, and Jesus Christ, whom you have sent' " (John 17:3). This "knowing" is not a merely intellectual acceptance but actual fellowship with God and Jesus, the *present* enjoyment of the blessing of a new quality of life— life eternal. This is characteristic of John.

**John's understanding of the love of God**
    Being the youngest of the twelve apostles, John opened his heart to Jesus with a childlike trust. His soul was touched by Jesus' teaching about representing God the Father. John came to see the essential difference between Jesus' nature and that of himself. Jesus had described him and his brother James as *Boanerges*—"sons of thunder"—because of their impetuous, intolerant nature (Mark 3:17). John and James once proposed calling fire from heaven to destroy those Samaritans who were disrespectful of Jesus (Luke 9:54). John also tried to stop a man who was casting out demons in Jesus' name because he did not belong to John's group (Luke 9:49). John and his brother even sought special honors and preference above the other apostles in the new kingdom (Mark 10:35-45). "At every possible opportunity, John took his place next to the Saviour, and James longed to be honored with as close connection with Him."[2]
    Jesus tried to purify the attachment of these brothers to Him. He saw it as "an outflowing from the fountain of His own redeeming love."[3] In place of their desire for a favorite position, He offered them a share in His suffering and death (Mark. 10:39). Ellen White explained this profoundly: "The one who stands nearest to Christ will

be he who on earth has drunk most deeply of the spirit of His self-sacrificing love."[4] Jesus kindly reproved the pride and ambition of John and James by indicating the fundamental difference between the rulers of the Gentiles and Himself—He had come to serve and to bless others (see Matt. 20:25-28).

Gradually, in the light of Jesus' love and compassion for others, John came to know himself better. "It is the revelation of God's love that makes manifest the deformity and sin of the heart centered in self."[5] John discovered that Jesus had not called him to authority but to service. He wanted to bring his life into harmony with the pattern of Jesus' life, and this—and the transforming power of Jesus' love—changed him more and more. John became known as "the disciple whom Jesus loved" (John 21:20). He felt Jesus' holy love so deeply in his heart that he "could talk of the Father's love as no other of the disciples could. . . . The glory of the Lord was expressed in his face."[6]

John received an even clearer concept of God's love when he witnessed Jesus' sufferings and crucifixion. He wrote: "This is how we know what love is: Jesus Christ laid down his life for us. And we ought to lay down our lives for our brothers" (1 John 3:16). God's self-giving love in Jesus became for John the unassailable source of his assurance of salvation: "How great is the love the Father has lavished on us, that we should be called children of God! And that is what we are!" (1 John 3:1). John fully realized that his love for God and Jesus Christ was only his *response* to the preceding love of God: "We love because he first loved us" (1 John 4:19).

He had no fear of the final judgment, no fear that it would endanger his assurance. He could face the day of judgment with full confidence "because in this world we are like him. There is no fear in love. But perfect love drives out fear, because fear has to do with punishment. The one who fears is not made perfect in love" (1 John 4:17, 18).

### The foundation of John's assurance

The fourth Gospel reveals that John based his certainty of faith and of salvation not on any virtue in himself but on Jesus' person and work. The following proclamation holds the central place in his Gospel:

The Word became flesh and made his dwelling among us. We have seen his glory, the glory of the One and Only, who came from the Father, full of grace and truth (John 1:14).

This passage has been called "the most crucial text in Holy Scripture" (Karl Barth). The incarnation of the Word of God determines the essential difference between Judaism and Christian faith, between a Torah-centered and a Christ-centered religion. When John stated that the Word of God "made his dwelling among us," or, literally, "tabernacled among us," he echoed Israel's tradition that Yahweh "dwelt" in the tabernacle in the wilderness. John's reference to Jesus' "glory" also connects with the ancient tabernacle, because that is where the "glory" of Yahweh resided (see Exod. 40:34, 35). John recognized that God's new dwelling is in Jesus' flesh. He saw God's glory and character manifested in Jesus of Nazareth—that is, not in any outward splendor but in the humble, earthly life of One who suffered rejection and a shameful death on a cross. Looking back from the end of the first century to Jesus' crucifixion and resurrection, John announced that Jesus' death was actually His finest hour, the "hour" of His "glorification" (see John 12:23-33; 13:31), because His death produced "many seeds" for eternity (John 12:24).

John did not build his spiritual security on any religious philosophy or ideology. He built on the undeniable, historical fact of the incarnated Word of God. He began his first letter with these words:

That which was from the beginning, which we have heard, which we have seen with our eyes, which we have looked at and our hands have touched—this we proclaim concerning the Word of life. The life appeared; we have seen it and testify to it, and we proclaim to you the eternal life, which was with the Father and has appeared to us (1 John 1:1, 2).

In chapter 1:14 of his Gospel, John expressed this appearance of the Word in the flesh by the term "one and only" [Greek: *monogenés*], translated as "the only begotten from the Father" (NASB) or as "a father's only son" (NRSV). The point is clear: Jesus is God's

Son in a unique way. What John wants to declare is that the eyewitnesses have experienced the fullness of divine grace in Christ: "From the fullness of his grace we have all received one blessing after another" (John 1:16). This can better be experienced than explained. Leon Morris commented: "God's grace to His people is continuous and is never exhausted. Grace knows no interruption and no limit. . . . Grace means an ever-deepening experience of the presence and the blessing of God."[7]

The cross of Christ, however, is not self-explanatory. It needs interpretation because it can be understood in different ways. Even the statement in John 3:16 can be misread as saying merely that God gave His Son to visit humankind with a revelation of God's goodness and goodwill for us. This inadequate understanding had already arisen in John's time, among the Gnostic Christians. He therefore wrote a special letter to explain more specifically the nature of God's love and the purpose of Jesus' death:

> This is love: not that we loved God, but that he loved us and sent his Son *as an atoning sacrifice [hilasmos]* for our sins (1 John 4:10, emphasis added).

John expressed Jesus' mission with the Greek word *hilasmos,* which literally means "propitiation" (see NASB). The New Revised Standard Version translates appropriately: "and sent his Son to be the atoning sacrifice for our sins" (1 John 4:10). John declared that Jesus "is the atoning sacrifice" for the sins of the whole world (1 John 2:2). John believed that God demonstrated His love in the sacrificial death of His Son. Jesus fulfilled the atoning sacrifices in Israel's temple cultus because He—the God-sent "Lamb of God"—actually took away the sins of the world (see John 1:29). Jesus died as the real Passover Lamb so that the judgment of God would "pass over" His covenant people (see Exod. 12:13). We can also grasp the significance of Jesus' death from the Messianic prophecy about the Servant of Yahweh who was led to the slaughter "like a lamb" (see Isaiah 53:7, 10, and note Philip's explanation, Acts 8:30-35).

So we may consider 1 John 4:10 a clarification of John 3:16. It reassures us that God's redeeming love is anchored for all eternity in the cross of Christ. This is fundamental to John's understanding of the gospel of God.

**The three witnesses**

John concluded his first letter by stating:

> This is the one who came by water and blood—Jesus Christ. He did not come by water only, but by water and blood. And it is the Spirit who testifies, because the Spirit is the truth. For there are three that testify: the Spirit, the water and the blood; and the three are in agreement. We accept man's testimony, but God's testimony is greater because it is the testimony of God, which he has given about his Son. Anyone who believes in the Son of God has this testimony in his heart. Anyone who does not believe God has made him out to be a liar, because he has not believed the testimony God has given about his Son (1 John 5:6-10).

John declared that the Incarnation and the Messiahship of Jesus, initiated at Jesus' baptism (the "water") and completed in His death (the "blood"), form the historic foundation of our salvation. John R. W. Stott offered this helpful comment:

> If the Son of God did not take to Himself our nature in His birth and our sins in His death, He cannot reconcile us to God. So John emphasizes not just that He *came*, but especially that He came by water and *blood*, since it is His blood which cleanses from sin (i. 7).[8]

The Holy Spirit testified to the divine Sonship of Jesus at His baptism (Matt. 3:16, 17) and throughout His ministry (Matt. 17:5; 12:28). So, in 1 John 5:8, John mentioned the Spirit as God's first witness. God's witness is superior to the testimony of human beings because God cannot lie and is more qualified than any creature to testify about Christ Jesus. Those who reject God's testimony about

Jesus reject God Himself. This is the ultimate manifestation of unbelief and guilt.

John also appealed to the believer's inner witness to the validity of belief in Jesus' divinity: "Anyone who believes in the Son of God has this testimony in his heart" (1 John 5:10). This parallels Paul's statement that "the Spirit himself testifies with our spirit that we are God's children" (Rom. 8:16). John insisted that all believers in Jesus have received an *anointing* of the Spirit of God and therefore know the truth (1 John 2:20, 27). He said, "We know it by the Spirit he gave us" (1 John 3:24), and "We know that we live in him and he in us, because he has given us his Spirit" (1 John 4:13). This is the confirming assurance from God in the believer's heart.

In summary, John pointed out that the Christian has *two* distinct assurances of salvation: God's testimony that Jesus is His own Son and the divine confirmation of such trust in the believer's heart. John's letter shows that faith in God and faith in Jesus cannot be separated. Faith in the Father is valid only when faith in the Son is maintained (see also John 5:22, 23). John addressed the false claims of some contemporary church members who denied that the man Jesus was identical with the divine Christ (1 John 4:2, 3). He declared: "No one who denies the Son has the Father; whoever acknowledges the Son has the Father also" (1 John 2:23).

Because God has guaranteed our eternal life in the Son, John could say: "He who has the Son has life; he who does not have the Son of God does not have life" (1 John 5:12). His point is, as in John 5:24, that eternal life is primarily qualitative rather than quantitative: "It is that highest *kind* of spiritual and moral life, irrespective of time, which God enables the believer to share in relationship with Jesus."[9] The testimony of God about His Son is that "God *has given* us eternal life, and this life is in his Son" (1 John 5:11, emphasis added). John's message is clear: "This letter is to assure you that you have eternal life" (1 John 5:13, NEB).

### The three tests of assurance

John considered faith in Jesus a commitment to Jesus that endures forever. Faith is entering into a covenant relationship with the

Lord for all eternity. It is walking with Him day by day, following Him with an undivided heart in grateful obedience to His will:

> We know that we have come to know him if we obey his commands. The man who says, "I know him," but does not do what he commands is a liar, and the truth is not in him. But if anyone obeys his word, God's love is truly made complete in him. This is how we know we are in him: Whoever claims to live in him must walk as Jesus did (1 John 2:3-6).

John particularly stressed Jesus' command *to love one another* (see John 13:34; 15:12; 1 John 2:7-11; 3:11). This was lacking in those who showed a spirit of superiority and exclusivity. John insisted that we must "*abide in him,* so that when he appears we may be confident and unashamed before him at his coming" (1 John 2:28, emphasis added). Ellen White also points to the necessity of a consistent walk with Jesus:

> Christ is our model. To copy Jesus, full of love and tenderness and compassion, will require that we draw near to Him daily. O how God has been dishonored by His professed representatives![10]

John maintained that Christian faith is not a set of abstract doctrines but a new moral life that accepts Jesus as *both* Redeemer and Example. John presented *three tests* that indicate with certainty that the believer truly knows Jesus and lives "in Him." These are, in the words of J. R. W. Stott: (1) the *moral* test of obedience; (2) the *social* test of love; and (3) the *doctrinal* test of belief in Christ.

John mentioned first that "if we claim to have fellowship with him [Jesus] yet walk in the darkness, we lie and do not live by the truth" (1 John 1:6; see also 2:4). He plainly stated that Jesus is also the Christian's moral standard of living. Claiming to be "in him" obliges us to "walk as Jesus did" (1 John 2:6). Stott said: "We cannot claim to abide in Him unless we behave like Him."[11] Jesus taught: " 'If you love me, you will obey what I command' " (John 14:15).

John added: "Everyone who has this hope in him purifies himself, just as he is pure" (1 John 3:3).

The second test is to walk in love with others. Jesus gave Moses' old commandment, "love your neighbor as yourself" (Lev. 19:18), a deeper meaning: " 'A new command I give you: Love one another. *As I have loved you, so you must love one another' "* (John 13:34, emphasis added). John explained: "If anyone says, 'I love God,' yet hates his brother, he is a liar. . . . Whoever loves God must also love his brother" (1 John 4:20, 21). Christian faith is validated when believers both obey God and love their brothers and sisters.

The final test is faithfulness to the unadulterated, apostolic gospel and its proclamation of Jesus as the incarnated Word of God. John urged all to "test the spirits to see whether they are from God, because many false prophets have gone out into the world" (1 John 4:1). John went so far as to state: "Who is the liar? It is the man who denies that Jesus is the Christ. Such a man is the antichrist—he denies the Father and the Son" (1 John 2:22; also 2 John 7). This means that "the fundamental doctrinal test of the professing Christian concerns his view of the Person of Jesus."[12] John declared that those who deny the deity of Jesus are not Christians. The seriousness of this denial of Jesus is that it implies a denial of God's own testimony. It is a denial of the Father *and* the Son!

In summary, John stressed two safeguards against error that were given in the beginning—*the apostolic Word and the anointing Spirit*, by which the believer may know for sure that he or she is *in* the truth and *in* Christ (see 1 John 1:1; 2:7, 27). Both gifts from God are needed to continue in the truth, to abide in Christ and to remain with conviction in the apostolic succession of the church.

---

1. D. A. Carson, *The Gospel According to John* (Grand Rapids, Mich.: Eerdmans, 1992), 95, 102.

2. E. G. White, *The Desire of Ages*, 548.

3. Ibid.

4. Ibid., 549.

5. Ibid., 498.

6. E. G. White, *The Acts of the Apostles*, 545.

7. Leon Morris, *The Gospel According to John* (Grand Rapids, Mich.: Eerdmans, 1977), 110, 111.

8. John R. W. Stott, *The Epistles of John,* Tyndale New Testament Commentary (Grand Rapids, Mich.: Eerdmans, 1976), 179.

9. S. S. Smalley, *1, 2, 3 John*, Word Biblical Commentary 51 (Waco, Tex.: Word Books, 1984), 287.

10. E. G. White, Letter 31a, 1894; cited in *SDA Bible Commentary,* 7:949.

11. Stott, 92.

12. Stott, 111.

*Chapter 8*

# Full Assurance of Faith in the Letter to the Hebrews

The letter to the Hebrews is probably the earliest sermon sent to the Jewish-Christian church in the city of Rome, where it became known first. The introduction of the New King James Version (1983) informs the reader: "Although the King James Version uses the title 'The Epistle of Paul the Apostle to the Hebrews,' there is no early manuscript evidence to support it [that title]. The oldest and most reliable title is simply *Pros Ebraious*, 'To Hebrews.' " The section in the NKJV entitled "The Author of Hebrews" presents six reasons why the majority of biblical scholars reject Pauline authorship of this letter but declares also: "The spiritual depth and quality of Hebrews bore witness to its inspiration, despite its anonymity." The church father Origen, who lived in the third century A.D., recognized that much of the letter to the Hebrews is of a Pauline character and presents the thoughts of Paul. Origen stated: "Therefore if any church holds that this epistle is by Paul, let it be commended for this."[1]

**The purpose of Hebrews**

Hebrews was most likely written between A.D. 64 and 68—that is, between the great fire of Rome and the suicide of Emperor Nero. During this time persecution against the Jewish Christians in Rome mounted. Some of them had forsaken the faith and were in danger of publicly renouncing their trust in Jesus (see 6:4-6; 10:26-31). Others had suffered hardship and loss because of their faith in Jesus (see 10:32-34).

Soon (in A.D. 70) the temple in Jerusalem with its old-covenant services would be destroyed. Thousands of Jewish Christians still worshiped in the temple, and all of them zealously upheld the law of Moses (see Acts 21:20). The letter to the Hebrews was addressed to a community in crisis, explaining the blessed truth of the heavenly sanctuary and the perfect High Priest of the new covenant that guaranteed a better hope than the old covenant had brought. M. L. Andreasen explained the urgent need for a new vision of Jesus' ministry:

> It is difficult for us to appreciate the crisis that faced the early church. The only thing that could save the people from bewilderment and discouragement when the Roman armies laid their beautiful temple in ruins was a clear conception of the true sanctuary and its services in heaven. . . . An understanding of the sanctuary was their salvation. Light on this vital subject must come to them if they were to triumph victoriously.[2]

The author of Hebrews sent this letter as "a word of exhortation" (13:22) intended to encourage the Jewish Christians to remain faithful to their commitment to Jesus, the Son of God. William G. Johnsson explained: "So the 'problem' of the Hebrew Christians is either a *weariness* leading to gradual drifting away from the community, or a deliberate, open *rejection* of Christ and His people because of the inroads of sin in the heart."[3] Some of these Jewish Christians were in danger of falling back into Judaism. Consequently, the pastorally oriented sermon had an intensely practical purpose: to urge loyalty to Jesus as the sole mediator of salvation and to warn of the judgment of God on indifference to the gospel message they had heard from the apostles.

William L. Lane states: "In moving language there is set forth the finality of God's revelation in His Son, whose transcendent dignity is superior both to the angels, who are ministering spirits (1:1-14), and to Moses, whose status was that of a servant in the household of faith (3:1-6)."[4] Lane points to *three contrasts* in Hebrews that demonstrate the superior dignity of Jesus as priest and sacrifice: (1) the temporal character of the Aaronic priesthood is contrasted with the eternal ministry of Jesus' priesthood (5:1-10; 7:1-28); (2) the Levitical priesthood of the old covenant is superseded by Jesus' priestly ministry in the heavenly sanctuary, establishing the new covenant (8:1-9:28); (3) the inadequacy of the sacrifices under the law is contrasted with the efficacy and finality of Jesus' sacrifice (10:1-18).

The author of Hebrews meant this theological reasoning to establish a firm foundation for his pastoral exhortation to readers. He intended his words to renew their sagging faith and faltering hope and to help them endure all suffering for Jesus' sake. He asked the pertinent question, *"How shall we escape if we neglect so great a salvation?"* (2:3). For that purpose, he centered his sermon on Jesus and His ongoing work of intercession, unfolding extensively the supremacy of Jesus' person (1:1-4:13) and the all-sufficiency of Jesus' work (4:14-10:18). He stressed that Christian faith is based on the unshakable Messianic promises of God and looks forward with absolute certainty to the promised future (see 11:1-40). Finally, he appealed to the supreme example of faith, Jesus Himself (12:1-3), as an incentive to steadfast endurance. So, the author moved from Jesus' person (1:1-4:13) to His work (4:14-10:18), and he concluded with an earnest appeal to persevere in Christian faith and love (10:19-13:25). Jesus' redemptive significance dominates all the thought patterns of this letter. No other biblical book sets Him forth so fully as our High Priest (see 2:17, 18; 4:14-5:10; 6:20-8:2).

## Full assurance in Jesus

We must have the benefits of a living faith in Jesus to enjoy assurance of faith and salvation. Hebrews mentions three substantial benefits:

> Therefore, brothers, since we have *confidence* [Greek: *parrêsia*] to enter the Most Holy Place by the blood of Jesus, by a new and living way opened for us through the curtain, that is, his body, and since we have a great priest over the house of God, let us draw near to God with a sincere heart *in full assurance* [Greek: *en plêrophoriai*] *of faith*, having our hearts sprinkled to cleanse us from a guilty conscience and having our bodies washed with pure water. Let us hold unswervingly to the hope we profess, for he who promised is faithful (10:19-23).

Christian assurance of faith and salvation rests on: (1) trust in the power of Jesus' blood, by which we have confidence to enter the heavenly sanctuary; (2) our great high priest in heaven; (3) and hearts or consciences cleansed from guilt before God. These affirmations, which enlarge those in 4:14-16, show how deeply rooted is Christian assurance in Jesus' present ministry in the heavenly sanctuary. This passage also states that Jesus' person and work have achieved our eternal security, surpassing all that came before. And it tells us that our assurance does not rest on our feelings but on Jesus! Here we find the answer to all doubts and feelings of guilt and of shortcomings. The certainty of our salvation does not depend on us or on what God thinks of us but on what God thinks of Jesus, our Substitute. Johnsson rightly stresses,

> Not in us but in Him. Not in who we are but in who He is. Not in what we have done but in what He has done. There lies our confidence, our assurance. *He* is our assurance.[5]

This good news motivates us and obliges us to continue to live by faith: "Let us hold *unswervingly* to the hope we profess, for he who promised is faithful" (10:23). Believers also bear responsibility. They must exercise faith daily and so develop *persevering* faith. Faith in the trustworthy promises of God must pierce through the clouds of doubt and lay hold of the risen Lord: "We have this hope as an anchor for the soul, *firm and secure*. It enters the inner sanctuary behind the curtain, where Jesus, who went before us, has entered on our behalf" (6:19, 20, emphasis added).

A promise is only as good as the one who makes it. We can trust promises that God makes because God Himself guarantees them. Our hope for the future is a trustworthy hope because its content is based on God's Word.

Even now in our hearts we can "taste," or experience, the powers of the future kingdom of God (see 6:5). Jesus delivers us from bondage to the fear of death because He "tasted" death "for everyone" (2:9) and set us free from "him who holds the power of death—that is, the devil" (2:14, 15).

## Our abiding need of assurance

Exhortation dominates Hebrews, as can be seen in 2:1-4; 3:7–4:16; 5:11–6:12; 10:19-39; and chapters 12 and 13. This letter has an intensely practical purpose. The inspired writer exhorts Jewish Christians—and by extension, all believers—to retain the courage and hope in Jesus that they profess (see 3:6). He warns them not to repeat the experience of Israel at Kadesh, in the desert of Paran, where the people hardened their hearts against God (3:7-19; see Num. 14).

This comparison of the Christian community with ancient Israel under Moses rests on the assumption that Israel and the church participate in a continuous history of redemption. God has constituted both Israel and the church by an act of revelation. In this unity of redemptive history, the relationship of Israel to the church is that of *type to antitype*. The author's typological interpretation of Psalm 95:7-11 plays a key role in the exhortation in Hebrews. Lane states: "The theology of rest developed in 4:1-11 takes account of the pattern of archetype (God's primal rest, 4:4), type (the settlement of Canaan under Joshua, 4:8), and antitype (the Sabbath celebration of the consummation, 4:9)."[6]

These historical correspondences grow out of the unity of God's plan of creation and salvation and that of the old and the new covenants. The same hope and conditions of divine grace are promised to all God's people. Psalm 95:7-11 provides an inspired meditation on Israel's history of rebellion (cp. Numbers 14). What was written concerning Israel's desert generation centuries earlier also has relevance to the church (Heb. 3:7).

The author wrote "Today, if you hear his voice, do not harden your hearts as you did in the rebellion, during the time of testing in the desert" (Heb. 3:7, 8) to remind each generation of God's people that they have the awesome responsibility to believe and to obey the voice of God. Entrance into the Promised Land still faces the conditions of active faith that responds to the promise of God and finds expression in obedience and endurance. Lane comments:

> The writer does not compare Christian existence to a long period of wandering in the desert but to the situation of a people whose pilgrimage was almost over and who were on the verge of

attaining what God had promised. The eschatological conviction of the writer is that Christians stand in a comparable situation with respect to entrance into God's rest. The basis of the comparison at Kadesh and the Christian community addressed is the unresolved tension of standing before the promise of God in a moment conditioned by trials and peril.[7]

The correspondence of the spiritual condition of Israel and that of the church forcefully teaches that forfeiture of the promised rest comes not as the result of an uncertain promise but because of unbelief and rebellion against the word of God. Hebrews assures us that Israel's failure to enter the promised rest did *not* abrogate the promise and the accessibility of that rest. The writer concluded: "Therefore, since the promise of entering his rest still stands, let us be careful that none of you be found to have fallen short of it" (4:1). We may retain our assurance of salvation by growing "to maturity" (6:1); that is, by moving forward to an adult understanding of Christ's present ministry and by enjoying "the full experience of salvation" (6:9, J. B. Phillips).

## Serious warnings against apostasy

Hebrews contains three severe warnings against falling away from faith in Jesus: 6:4-6, 10:26-31, and 12:15-17. Johnsson perceives here a parallel with the third angel's message of Revelation 14:9-12 "in its apparent uncompromising stance."[8] It is important to notice the "if" in Hebrews 6:6, which indicates the real danger of apostasy. The writer is not dealing here with the occasional lapse of faith or with shortcomings that result from our weak nature. The author speaks of "crucifying the Son of God all over again and subjecting him to public disgrace" (6:6). In a radical contrast, he combines words of Christian assurance with serious warnings of the consuming fire of God's judgment. He sharply contrasts two eternal destinies.

The same contrast characterized the message of John the Baptist: "Whoever believes in the Son has eternal life, but whoever rejects the Son will not see life, for God's wrath remains on him" (John 3:36). This contrast also appears in the threefold message of Revelation 14, which prepares the final generation for the Second Advent (see verses 6-12).

That passage unites the offer of the eternal gospel to all people with the stern warning of the consuming wrath of God.

For the Jewish-Christian communities during the rule of Nero, the danger of publicly renouncing Jesus was not merely hypothetical. It called for the gravest possible warning. This fits the severe warning to Christians in Hebrews 6:4-6. In view are those who have experienced the reality of personal salvation—"who have once been enlightened, who have tasted the heavenly gift, who have shared in the Holy Spirit, who have tasted the goodness of the word of God and the powers of the coming age" (6:4, 5). Lane comments: "Accordingly, in vv 4-5 the writer identifies the congregation as witnesses to the fact that God's salvation and presence are the unquestionable reality of their lives."[9] The words of Hebrews 6:4, 5 describe a full and authentic Christian experience.

The inspired author declared that if such believers "fall away," they cannot "be brought back to repentance" (6:4, 6). To apprehend the seriousness of the situation, we need to understand the nature of this "apostasy." Lane clarifies: "Apostasy entailed a decisive rejection of God's gifts, similar to the rejection of the divine promise by the Exodus generation at Kadesh (3:7-4:2)."[10] The author does not tell us what form the Hebrews' apostasy took other than saying that they were "crucifying the Son of God all over again and subjecting him to public disgrace" (6:6). In the light of their baptismal confession about Jesus as the Son of God in 4:14, the threat was to deny His deity. Lane explains, "This could entail a return to Jewish convictions and practices as well as the public denial of faith in Christ under pressure from the magistrate or a hostile crowd, simply for personal advantage (cf. Mark 8:34-38)."[11] The letter to the Hebrews says that to repudiate Jesus publicly is to reject the Holy Spirit, making it "impossible" to come to repentance (see Acts 5:31).

The agricultural illustration in Hebrews 6:7, 8 clarifies the warning in verses 4-6, as the connecting word "for" [Greek: *gar*] in verse 7 indicates (unfortunately omitted in the NIV). The writer compares the Christian community with land that has received frequent rain and the blessing of God (6:7). This recalls God's covenant with Israel in Deuteronomy 11:11, 12. If Christians fall away from Jesus, they become like a field that was well watered but produced only "thorns and thistles" (6:8). This last phrase clearly alludes to Genesis 3:17, 18, which identifies the growth

of thorns and thistles as the consequence of the curse on human disobedience. The motif of blessing (Heb. 6:7) and curse (6:8) places the entire
warning of Hebrews 6:4-6 firmly in a *covenantal* context (see also Deut.
11:26-28).

The subsequent words in verse 9 confirm the writer's confidence
that God has given Christian believers, his "dear friends," indisputable
evidence of the blessings of salvation. He expects them to remain active
in Christian love "to the very end, in order to make your hope sure"
(6:11). This is the practical concern of the letter to the Hebrews.

## The basis for Christian confidence and perseverance

In Hebrews 6 the author turns from exhortation to a discussion of
the reliability of God's promise extended to Christians through the high-
priestly ministry of Christ. He sets forth the absolute certainty and reliability of God's promise. God gave humanity a twofold assurance, as He
demonstrated to Abraham. He gave them His promise and then His sol-
emn oath. Abraham received the promise and God's confirming oath
after having been severely tested both in faith and endurance (6:13-15;
see Gen. 22). The following words stress the legal significance of the
divine promise: "Because God wanted to make the unchanging nature
of his purpose very clear to the heirs of what was promised, he confirmed it with an oath" (6:17). The divine oath provides the guarantee
that excludes any doubt about the abiding validity of the promise.

The writer mentions Abraham as the example of faith and endurance whom all Christians must emulate. Hebrews extends the promis-
sory oath of God to Christian believers, with an appeal to the Messianic
promise in Psalm 110:4 (see Heb. 5:6; 6:20). The promise to Abraham
expresses also God's unalterable will for them: "God did this so that, by
two unchangeable things in which it is impossible for God to lie, *we* who
have fled to take hold of the hope offered to *us* may be greatly encouraged. *We* have this hope as an anchor for the soul, firm and secure"
(6:18, 19, emphasis added). The hope that Christians "take hold of" is
the objective gift that God extends to His people through Jesus. In Hebrews, the word *hope* describes "the objective content of hope, consist-
ing of present and future salvation."[12]

The promise to Abraham prefigures the salvation God has given the Christian people because Jesus is the Son of God. As the appointed High Priest, He has entered now "on our behalf" into God's presence *"behind the veil"* in the heavenly sanctuary (6:20). The expression "behind the veil" stands parallel to these words: "He entered heaven itself, now to appear for us in God's presence" (9:24). Adventist Bible scholars state that "there is nothing here that would identify the veil with which we are dealing, but *katapetasma* ['veil'] is introduced simply to locate where Jesus is ministering—the place where the hope of the covenant people is centered and from whence the covenant blessings are dispensed." They conclude, consequently, that the author of Hebrews used "the veil" metaphorically for the sanctuary in heaven.[13]

The new covenant offers this blessing: that through the risen Lord all Christians now have *direct access to God* in priestly service (10:22; see also Rom. 5:2). Christ Jesus anchors the Christian's hope. "His person and His work make our salvation absolutely sure."[14]

---

1. In W. G. Johnsson, *Hebrews*, The Abundant Life Bible Amplifier, G. R. Knight, ed. (Nampa, Idaho: Pacific Press, 1994), 25.

2. M. L. Andreasen, *The Book of Hebrews* (Hagerstown, Md.: Review and Herald, 1948), 38.

3. Johnsson, 21.

4. William L. Lane, *Hebrews 1–8*, Word Biblical Commentary 47a (Dallas, Tex.: Word Books, 1991), c.

5. Johnsson, 192.

6. Lane, cxxiii.

7. Ibid., 90.

8. Johnsson, 114.

9. Lane, 142.

10. Ibid.

11. Ibid.

12. Ibid., 153.

13. G. E. Rice, in *Issues in the Book of Hebrews*, Daniel & Revelation Commentary Series (Silver Spring, Maryland: Biblical Research Institute, 1989), 4:234; see also H. Kiesler, ibid., 76.

14. Johnsson, 119.

*Chapter 9*

# Surrounded by a Host of Witnesses

The letter to the Hebrews encourages Christian believers "to imitate those who through faith and patience [Greek: *makrothumia*, "longsuffering"] inherit what has been promised" (6:12). It explains the specific need of the believers in more detail:

> Do not throw away your confidence; it will be richly rewarded. You need to persevere [Greek: *hypomonê*, "endurance"] so that when you have done the will of God, you will receive what he has promised (10:35, 36).

The author bolsters this appeal for perseverance or endurance by citing the classic assurance of Habakkuk that promised survival in Jerusalem's coming crisis to all who lived by their faith: *"But my righteous one will live by faith"* (10:38; Hab. 2:4). The author of Hebrews applies Habakkuk 2:4 to Christian believers who may doubt if Jesus will ever return according to His promise. If they persevere in their faith, they will gain life eternal. If they relapse from their Christian profession into their earlier way of life, they will prove themselves reprobate. The writer concludes: *"We* are not of those who shrink back and are destroyed, but of *those who believe and are saved"* (10:39, emphasis added). F. F. Bruce translated the last words as "we maintain our faith and win through to life."[1]

The appeal for steadfast endurance returns in chapter 12, where we read: "Let us run with perseverance [Greek: *hypomonê*, "endurance"] the race marked out for us. Let us fix our eyes on Jesus, the author and perfecter of our faith, who for the joy set before him endured the cross, scorning its shame, and sat down at the right hand on the throne of God" (12:1, 2).

A pilgrim motif apparently serves as the organizing idea of the letter to the Hebrews. For ancient Israel, pilgrimage had the distinctive characteristics of separation, hardship, and goal. The author of Hebrews intended to reactivate the faith of Christians in a crisis situation by presenting some inspiring examples of faith from earlier days. For that reason he developed the large "faith-chapter" (11), which lists some outstanding men and women who demonstrated their faith in the promises of God through acts of obedience and endurance. "Christians are to recognize in those who acted upon God's promises, even though fulfillment was not in sight, a standard of persevering faith worthy of emulation."[2]

### The essence of faith

The author began this chapter by defining the *nature* of the faith of some attested witnesses of the past: "Faith is being sure of what we hope for and certain of what we do not see" (11:1, NIV), or, "Faith is the assurance of things hoped for, the conviction of things not seen" (NRSV, NASB), or, "Faith is the realization of what is hoped for and evidence of things not seen" (NAB). In short, faith recognizes the reality of what is not seen and is now the object of hope. And hope is the forward-looking aspect of faith. This parallels Paul's description: "If we hope for what we do not yet have, we wait for it patiently [Greek: *hypomonê*]" (Rom. 8:25). So, faith and hope presuppose the promise of God, as Paul affirmed: *"Faith comes from hearing the message,* and the message is heard through the word of Christ" (Rom. 10:17, emphasis added).

Hebrews stresses the *persevering* nature of faith and hope in God's word. Of that faith the saints of the Old Testament gave a striking example (Heb. 11:1-40), as Bruce explains: "Their faith consisted simply in taking God at His word and directing their lives accordingly; things yet future so far as their experience went were thus present to faith, and things outwardly unseen were visible to the inward eye."[3] Faith is not a meritorious act but the organ that enables a person to "see" the invisible order of the future (as Moses did, 11:27). While faith is a gift of God (Eph. 2:8), it is humanity's responsibility to exercise it.

Hebrews is directed to redeemed believers. Their need was not to *become* Christians but to *continue* as Christians. They were suffering spiritual battle-fatigue, just as the ancient Israelites became weary and fell away in the wilderness (see 1 Cor. 10:1-10; Heb. 3:16-19). Hebrews encourages the struggling Christians to be faithful to their confession of faith, to endure steadfastly in a time of crisis, and to persevere as pilgrims en route to the heavenly Jerusalem: "For here we do not have an enduring city, but we are looking for the city that is to come" (13:14). This trust in God's word, expressed in obedient faithfulness, is the essence of a living faith. It was demonstrated in the lives of the champions of faith found in the biblical record.

### Attested witnesses

The author mentioned several figures from the Hebrew Scriptures who stand out as believers and whom God said were pleasing in His sight: Abel, Enoch, Noah, Abraham, Isaac, Jacob, Moses, and others (11:4-28). The author underscored the divine approval of their faith: "Without faith it is impossible to please God, because anyone who comes to him must believe that he exists and that he rewards those who earnestly seek him" (11:6). Hebrews highlights the relational aspect of saving faith when it specifies that to be genuine, faith must be directed "toward God" (6:1, NASB). True faith not only believes in God's existence but also that He is the "rewarder" of those who earnestly seek Him. "The firm expectation of the reward, then, is a matter of unwavering hope in the God who controls the future."[4]

God accepted Abel's offerings because of his faith and righteous life (11:4): "The LORD looked with favor on Abel and his offering" (Gen. 4:4; see also Matt. 23:35). Jewish tradition explained that fire fell from heaven and consumed Abel's offering, while Cain's offering remained untouched.[5] This testimony of Scripture teaches that God sees not only the appropriate sacrifice but primarily the heart and life of the giver (see the order in Gen. 4:4). "For the writer of

Hebrews it was axiomatic that the source of righteousness was faith (see 11:5-7)."[6]

Enoch received God's commendation "as one who pleased God" (11:5). The record states that "Enoch walked with God 300 years" after he became a father (Gen. 5:22). This indicates that Enoch received divine approval because he relied daily on God to help him be a good example to his children. Ellen White comments:

> Enoch's walk with God was not in a trance or a vision, but in all the duties of his daily life. He did not become a hermit, shutting himself entirely from the world; for he had a work to do for God in the world. In the family and in his intercourse with men, as a husband and father, a friend, a citizen, he was the steadfast, unwavering servant of the Lord.[7]

God gave Enoch prophetic visions, and he became a preacher of righteousness (see Jude 14, 15). He steadfastly maintained his communion with God through earnest prayers. But God's ultimate attestation of Enoch came when He translated him "by faith" into glory, "so that he did not experience death" (Heb. 11:5).

Hebrews mentions Noah as an example of faith, because "by faith" Noah built an ark to save his family (11:7). Saving faith, then, implies obedience to God's revelation of "things not yet seen." Noah's act dramatizes the essence of faith as defined in 11:1 and 6. Noah was counted as a righteous man in his generation (Gen. 6:9; 7:1); he "did everything just as God commanded him" (Gen. 6:22). Noah's willing obedience testified to the quality of his faith. And his faith witnessed effectively: "As a reward for his faithfulness and integrity, God saved all the members of his family with him. What encouragement to parental fidelity!"[8]

"By his faith [Noah] condemned the world and became heir of the righteousness that comes by faith" (11:7). This declaration has a Pauline ring! It declares that righteousness is bestowed by God through faith. Noah responded to God's word with a full measure of faith and conviction. At the same time, "through his faith he put the whole world in the wrong" (NEB). He accurately represented the biblical way of salvation: "My righteous one shall live by faith" (10:38).

   The author presents Abraham as his crown exemplar of faith. He devotes more space to this patriarch than to any other Old Testament figure (11:8-12, 17-19). He begins by reminding his readers of Abraham's call and departure from Mesopotamia:

> *By faith* Abraham, when called to go to a place he would later receive as his inheritance, obeyed and went, even though he did not know where he was going. *By faith* he made his home in the promised land like a stranger in a foreign country; he lived in tents, as did Isaac and Jacob, who were heirs of the same promise. *For he was looking forward to the city with foundations, whose architect and builder is God* (11:8-10, emphasis added; see Gen. 12:1, 8).

   The writer points out that Abraham's life demonstrated the correlation between faith and obedience (v. 8). The recurring phrase "by faith" means to say that "faith is the active response to the spoken word of God" (Lane). In this Abraham presents an exemplary witness to Christian believers. He left his homeland and family to go to the promised "inheritance" (v. 8). What Abraham understood to be his inheritance is of critical importance to Hebrews. It declares in 11:9, 10, 13-16 that it was *not* the land of Canaan but the city that God has prepared for His people. Here Hebrews differs from the tradition of Judaism and Zionism, which focus on the earthly land as the inheritance. Abraham *"was looking forward to the city with foundations whose architect and builder is God"* (v. 10, emphasis supplied). This hope was revealed by his continuous dwelling in tents that have no solid foundation. The patriarchs' practice of living in tents indicated that they were pilgrims and strangers. It indicated that Canaan was not, in the final sense, the promised inheritance. Hebrews clarifies this important point:

> All these people were still living by faith when they died. They did not receive the things promised; they only saw them and welcomed them from a distance. And they admitted that they were aliens and strangers on earth (11:13).

So, the patriarchs had an *apocalyptic hope*, because the city of God remains a future reality. Their faith looked forward, assuring them of what they could not see (see 11:1). They didn't hope for an abstract heavenly place but for a "city with foundations" (v. 10)—that is, a city that provides an unshakable and abiding home (see 12:28; 13:14), "the heavenly Jerusalem, the city of the living God" (12:22). The Apocalypse of Jesus Christ, in its vision of the Holy City, the New Jerusalem, "coming down out of heaven from God" (Rev. 21:2, 10-14, 19-20), details this hope.

After recounting more champions of faith, such as Sarah, Jacob, Joseph, and Moses, who "persevered because he saw him who is invisible" (v. 27), and many others, Hebrews 11 closes with a pastoral appeal: "God had planned something better for us so that only together with us would they be made perfect" (v. 40). This affirmation recognizes the sovereignty and grace of God. He decides that the Hebrew saints will attain ultimate salvation only in association with the people of the new covenant. Only when the saints of old experience "a better resurrection" (11:35) will they, *together with Christian believers,* enter the eternal inheritance (vs. 39, 40).

Hebrews makes it clear that the perfecting of faithful men and women under the old covenant depends on the substitutionary death of Jesus. The promised eternal inheritance will be given only by virtue of Christ's sacrifice (see 9:15). This assurance underlies a moving appeal to the wavering Christians:

> *Since we are surrounded by such a great cloud of witnesses,* let us throw off everything that hinders and the sin that so easily entangles, and let us run with perseverance the race marked out for us. Let us fix our eyes on Jesus, the author and perfecter of our faith, who for the joy set before him endured the cross, scorning its shame, and sat down at the right hand of God (12:1, 2, emphasis added).

The author realizes that he can expect an effective response only by appealing to the supreme example of persevering faith, Jesus Christ.

He raises Jesus before his readers to inspire heroic Christian discipleship that will endure hostile opposition and even martyrdom.

**The inspiring example of Job**

The letter of James likewise encourages Christian believers to "be patient and to stand firm, because the Lord's coming is near" (5:8). James presented the example of Job, who was patient in the face of suffering: "You have heard of Job's perseverance and have seen what the Lord finally brought about. The Lord is full of compassion and mercy" (5:11). James's words direct us to consider briefly Job's wonderful testimony, as recorded in his book.

Job may have suffered more than any other person the Old Testament names. The tragic circumstances of his life bewildered and discouraged him. He felt utterly forsaken and detested by all (Job 19:13-20). His experience defied any logical or theological explanation, and it led him to the brink of utter despair. He found his eloquent friends "miserable comforters" (Job 16:1) who failed to provide the needed explanation.

But in all his bitter darkness, Job held on to his integrity and to his trust in God's justice (27:1-6). The explanation of his experience must come from God Himself (12:13). In remarkable words, Job declared: "Though he slay me, *yet will I hope in him. . . . I know I will be vindicated*" (13:15, 18, emphasis added). He saw his sufferings not as a punishment, as his friends did, but as a divine testing that he accepted with unwavering confidence (23:10). With tears he expressed the certainty of his faith: " 'Even now my witness is in heaven; my advocate is on high. My intercessor is my friend as my eyes pour out tears to God' " (16:19-20).

Job did not claim sinless perfection but simply declared his innocence against the false accusations of his fundamentalist friends (chapter 31). His challenge was: " 'Let God weigh me in honest scales and he will know that I am blameless' " (31:6). His struggles were those of a sincere believer. He wished that his words of self-vindication were written on a scroll, " 'inscribed with an iron tool on lead, or engraved in rock forever!' " as his testimony that would remain after his death (see 19:23, 24). And Job spoke of his unshakable faith:

"I know that my Redeemer [or "Defender," NIV (margin); or "Vindicator," NEB] lives, and that in the end he will stand upon the earth [or, "upon my grave," NIV(margin)]. And after my skin has been destroyed, yet in my flesh I will see God; I myself will see him with my own eyes—I, and not another" (19:25-27).

Job was convinced that his stay in the grave would be only temporary (see also 14:13, 14) and that God would not abandon him but be his Vindicator in the heavenly court on his behalf (see the NEB in Job 19:25-27). In addition, this passage shows that Job believed that though he might die, his life and personality would be restored. Francis I. Andersen states: "The hope of resurrection lies at the very heart of Job's faith."[9]

Ellen G. White captures Job's amazing assurance of the triumph of divine justice in the face of his rejection and despair in these words: "From the depths of discouragement and despondency Job rose to the heights of implicit trust in the mercy and the saving power of God."[10] What an inspiring example, calling all persecuted, suffering believers to persevere till the end!

## Songs of assurance in the Psalms

Different authors in the book of Psalms testify to their full confidence in the God of Israel. They sing in poetic form about the protection and provision of their covenant God who will never abandon them in their hour of need. They commit themselves to His care and faithfulness.

David praised the Lord with perfect assurance while facing the threat of death:

LORD, you have assigned me my portion and my cup; you have made my lot secure. The boundary lines have fallen for me in pleasant places; surely I have a delightful inheritance. . . . I have set the LORD always before me. Because he is at my right hand, I will not be shaken. . . . You will fill me with joy in your presence, with eternal pleasures at your right hand (Ps. 16:5, 6, 8, 11).

David's assurance in the face of mortal danger was founded on the fact that the faithful covenant God was always before him in daily prayers (v. 8). He rejoiced in God's deliverance from an untimely death and in experiencing the joy of life in God's presence (vs. 9-11).

Psalm 16 remains an inspiration for all who are shaken by a fear of death. P.C. Craigie comments, "It is a fear which must be controlled confidently if life is to be lived fully, yet it is a fear which can never be controlled absolutely. Yet its sting is removed in the new meaning of Ps. 16: the terminal threat of Sheol [death] was conquered in the resurrection of Jesus."[11]

Psalm 23 is undoubtedly one of the most endearing songs of assurance. It functioned originally in the context of some ritual of thanksgiving (see vs. 5, 6). David presented the essentials of faith in terms of a relationship between a shepherd and his sheep. He called God his personal Shepherd who provides protection in the present and security for the future:

> The LORD is my shepherd, I shall not be in want. . . . He restores my soul. He guides me in paths of righteousness, for his name's sake. Even though I walk through the valley of the shadow of death, I will fear no evil, for you are with me; your rod and your staff, they comfort me (vs. 1-4).

David declared: "So long as the Lord is my shepherd, I suffer no lack." This resembles Moses' words about the wandering Israelites after the Exodus: "And you have not lacked anything" (Deut. 2:7). David also spoke about the guidance and strength that God will continue to give him. He based this confidence on the bedrock of Israel's experience with God during their journey in the wilderness. As God was able to "spread a table in the desert" (see Ps. 78:19, 20), so David was convinced "You prepare a table before me in the presence of my enemies. . . . My cup overflows. Surely goodness and love [Hebrew: *hesed*, "steadfast love"] will follow me all the days of my life, and I will dwell in the house of the LORD forever" (23:5, 6).

David's faith-inspiring experience of the past and the joy of the present gave rise to his magnificent expression of confidence in the future in verse 6. David trusted implicitly the covenant God who in the past had so bountifully shown His lovingkindness [*hesed*] to His people by redeeming them. The same God will redeem all who follow Him as their Shepherd. When Jesus said " 'I am the good Shepherd' " (John 10:11), He claimed to represent Israel's God for all who accept Him as the divine Messiah. He laid down His life for His sheep so that they will receive a crown of eternal glory (see Heb. 13:20; 1 Pet. 5:4). We can trust our souls to this good Shepherd.

1. F. F. Bruce, *The Epistle to the Hebrews* (London: Marshall, 1971), 275.

2. W. L. Lane, *Hebrews 9–13*, Word Biblical Commentary 47b (Dallas, Tex.: Word Books, 1991), 313.

3. F. F. Bruce, 277.

4. W. L. Lane, 338.

5. See Theodotion's translation of Genesis 4:4, 5; see also E. G. White, *Patriarchs and Prophets*, 71.

6. W. L. Lane, 335.

7. E. G. White, *Patriarchs and Prophets,* 85.

8. Ibid., 98.

9. Francis I. Andersen, *Job* (Downers Grove, Ill.: InterVarsity Press, 1992), 194.

10. E. G. White, *Prophets and Kings*, 163.

11. P. C. Craigie, *Psalms 1–50*, Word Biblical Commentary 19 (Dallas, Tex.: Word Books, 1983), 158, 159.

## Chapter 10

# Assurance and the Final Judgment

Some have argued that the doctrine of justification by faith is incompatible with a final judgment according to works. The biblical relationship between justification and sanctification provides the most important key to understanding this issue. The best illustration represents justification as the *root* and sanctification the *fruit* of salvation. If the believer's assurance of salvation rests on God's gift of justification alone, the sanctified life does not provide any part of our assurance of salvation.

To refresh your memory, you may benefit from rereading chapter 5, "Paul's Assurance of Salvation." You find there that Ellen White called justification our "title to heaven" and sanctification our "fitness for heaven." One cannot have title to heaven while rejecting the transforming fitness for that holy place. But what do the Scriptures say—the New Testament in particular? Did Jesus and the apostles consider justification by faith and judgment according to works mutually exclusive?

To everyone who accepts Jesus as a personal Savior, He issues the call to *discipleship*. In His final commission to His apostles He said: " 'Go and *make disciples of all nations*, baptizing them in the name of the Father and of the Son and of the Holy Spirit, and *teaching them to obey everything I have commanded you*' " (Matt. 28:19, 20, emphasis added).

While the fruits of our redeemed life must be visible and expressed in a new relationship with Jesus and with our fellow humans, however, such fruits do not constitute the basis of our eternal life. Paul explained: "The only thing that counts is *faith expressing itself through love*" (Gal. 5:6, emphasis added). Such a living faith demonstrates through newness of life that Jesus is our salvation. He cannot be restricted to justification *or* sanctification *or* glorification. In Him we receive both present and future salvation. The issue hinges on one question only: whether one abides in Jesus. He taught this in His parable of the vine and the branches (John 15:1-8). This parable is of critical importance for our present theme. It contains the crucial aspect of judgment for all who have entered into a faith-relation with Him.

Jesus said:

> "I am the vine; you are the branches. If a man remains in me and I in him, he will bear much fruit; apart from me you can do nothing. If anyone does not remain in me, he is like a branch that is thrown away and withers; such branches are picked up, thrown into the fire and burned. . . . If you obey my commands, you will remain in my love, just as I have obeyed my Father's commands and remain in his love" (John 15:5, 6, 10).

This parable teaches that we do not automatically "remain" in Christ Jesus. Instead, faith brings a personal responsibility to renew that relationship day by day. Those who do bear "much fruit." Jesus wants us to remain in Him because apart from Him we can do "nothing"—that is, we can do nothing acceptable to God. Without Jesus, we cannot overcome temptation and sin. And Jesus taught that the final judgment will assess believers regarding their "remaining" in Him!

Jesus equated forgiveness of sins with justification when He said of the repentant tax collector, " 'I tell you that this man, rather than the other, went home *justified* before God' " (Luke 18:14, emphasis added). He equated this justification with salvation when He said to Zacchaeus, the repentant tax collector, " 'Today salvation has come to this house' " (Luke 19:9). On the other hand, Jesus also taught that at His second advent He would come as the Judge and " 'then he will reward each person according to what he has done' " (Matt. 16:27). To the surprise of many Jews, He even declared that " 'the subjects of the kingdom [the nominal covenant people of God] will be thrown outside, into the darkness, where there will be weeping and gnashing of teeth' " (Matt. 8:11). To Jesus, the final judgment meant the eternal separation of the saved from the unsaved, of the righteous from the hypocrites. Such a separation would not be left to the church or her leaders but to the angels of Christ alone " 'at the end of the age!' " (Matt. 13:40-43, 49, 50).

Jesus repeated His teaching on the final judgment several times (see Matt. 22:11-13; 24:50, 51; 25:30), especially in His parable of the sheep and the goats (Matt. 25:31-46). Those who lacked all mercy for needy people will receive their share with " 'the devil and his angels' " (Matt. 25:41-46). The righteous, however, do their good deeds on behalf of the needy as the natural expression of their love for Jesus (Matt. 25:35-40) and not as the basis of their glorification. They cannot earn the kingdom of God; they can only inherit it! " 'Then the King will say to those on his right, "Come, you who are blessed by my Father, take *your inheritance*, the kingdom *prepared for you since the creation of the world* " ' " (Matt. 25:34, emphasis added). Salvation is based on God's grace, appropriated by faith in Jesus alone. The saved are therefore called "His elect;" that is, those Jesus has chosen (see Matt. 24:31).

## Paul's theology of justification and judgment

To avoid misrepresenting Paul's teaching we must pay careful attention to his theology of salvation. While Paul centered his gospel on justification by faith, he included the final judgment in his gospel. Paul's teaching on justification and the final judgment continues that of the Old Testament. He appealed to Moses, the Psalms, and the Prophets as the Hebrew pillars of his apostolic gospel (see Rom. 4:3, 6-8; Gal. 3:11), acknowledging an essential unity of both Testaments regarding salvation, both present and future. As God was at the same time Israel's King, Savior, Lawgiver, and Judge (see Isa. 33:22), so is Jesus "our righteousness, holiness, and redemption" (1 Cor. 1:30). Paul added:

> We must all appear before the judgment seat of Christ, that
> each one may receive what is due him for the things done
> while in the body, whether good or bad (2 Cor. 5:10).

Paul stressed that "God does not show favoritism" (Rom. 2:11;
Eph. 6:9) and that "God does not judge by external appearance" (Gal.
2:6). He said that "anyone who does wrong will be repaid for his
wrong, and there is no favoritism" (Col. 3:25). The final judgment
doesn't play a secondary role in Paul's preaching. On the contrary, he
believed the final judgment will consider humanity's works and actions (see also 1 Cor. 3:12-15; 4:5; Gal. 6:7-9). God will judge
according to the actual quality of humankind's existence and not according to any favoritism for a special covenant people. Paul stated
this idea forcefully in his letter to the Christians in Rome:

> God "will give to each person according to what he has done."
> To those who by persistence in doing good seek glory, honor
> and immortality, he will give eternal life. But for those who
> are self-seeking and who reject the truth and follow evil, there
> will be wrath and anger (Rom. 2:6-8).

Paul's teaching of *both* justification by faith and judgment
according to works should call our attention to the close correlation between faith and works. He distinguished sharply between
*works of faith* (1 Thess. 1:3; Gal. 5:6) and *works of the law* or
merit-seeking before God (Gal. 3:10). Paul saw no contrast between faith and works, only between faith and law-righteousness
(Gal. 2:16, 21). The decisive factor is whether or not human works
are done from faith: "Everything that does not come from faith is
sin" (Rom. 14:23). So the theological contrast is not between an
abstract faith and human acts but between "works of faith" and
"works of the law," or self-righteous works (see Phil. 3:7-9). This
understanding does not mean that Paul argued for salvation through
faith *plus* works. He advocated instead faith *that works!* This dis-

tinction stands true also of the final judgment.

Paul did not regard faith as merely an opinion. Instead, he saw it as a living relationship with Jesus, an embracing of Jesus that imparts the Holy Spirit and transforms the soul, filling it with the merciful love of God that engenders a new life (Gal. 3:2, 5). The Spirit of Christ motivates this new life: "The fruit of the Spirit is love, joy, peace, patience, kindness, goodness, faithfulness, gentleness and self-control" (Gal. 5:22, 23).

Whether or not one does the will of God reveals whether one's faith is real or merely intellectual conviction, merely saying "Lord, Lord." Ellen White explained: "We want that living faith which grasps the arm of infinite power, and we want to rely with all our being upon Jesus Christ, our righteousness. And we may do it. Yes, we do it profitably to our own soul's interest."[1]

Such a faith is demonstrated in good works, as Jesus taught: " 'A tree is recognized by its fruit' " (Matt. 12:33). These "works" have nothing to do with the "works of the law" or with self-righteousness. The "righteous" ones are not aware of their good deeds toward the needy. They reply with astonishment, " ' "Lord, when did we see *you* hungry and feed *you*, or thirsty and give *you* something to drink?" ' " (Matt. 25:37, emphasis added). Jesus explained that the good works of His redeemed followers are counted as done to Him! This vital connection between faith and Jesus lies at the foundation of all the ethical imperatives in the New Testament. When Paul had completed his exposition of righteousness by faith in his letter to the church in Rome (chapters 1–11), he continued with this moral appeal: *"Therefore,* I urge you, brothers, *in view of God's mercy,* to offer your bodies as living sacrifices, holy and pleasing to God—this is your spiritual act of worship" (Rom. 12:1, emphasis added).

The Reformed theologian G. C. Berkouwer concluded with true perception: "The judgment according to works, seen in its depths, is therefore a decision about faith and unbelief."[2] Works *by themselves* do not decide the outcome of the final judgment. Rather, it is the relation of these works to Jesus and to His saving grace that is crucial. God alone can determine whether our works are done from faith and to the honor of God.

Jesus indicated the value of a work acceptable to God when He said of the woman who anointed Him with expensive perfume in Simon's house: " 'She has done a beautiful thing *to me*' " (Matt. 26:10, emphasis added). The Lord's Prayer also indicates the connection between faith and works: " 'If you forgive men when they sin against you, your heavenly Father will also forgive you. But if you do not forgive men their sins, your Father will not forgive your sins' " (Matt. 6:14, 15).

Jesus illustrated the serious consequence of our willingness or unwillingness to forgive others in His parable of the unmerciful servant. He concluded: " 'This is how my heavenly Father will treat each of you unless you forgive your brother from your heart' " (Matt. 18:35). The point is not that believers must manifest a general virtue of forgiving others but that they should show the same mercy to others that they have received from the Redeemer: " ' "Shouldn't you have had mercy on your fellow servant just as I had on you?" ' " (Matt. 18:33). So the believer's spirit of forgiveness is a token of God's grace, a reflection of God's own forgiveness, and this is decisive in the final judgment.

Performing great works such as prophesying or doing miracles or exorcising demons in Jesus' name will not guarantee one's standing in the final judgment. Jesus warned that He will say of some who do these works: " ' "I never knew you. Away from me, *you evildoers!*" ' " (Matt. 7:23, emphasis added). In short, judgment according to works clashes not with justification by faith but with a life of lawlessness. God appointed Jesus the Judge of the world (Acts 17:31). Because He is both our Redeemer and our Lord, our Substitute *and* our Example, justification *and* judgment according to works are united in perfect harmony in Him. Ivan T. Blazen stated it well:

> In terms of the actual data of Scripture, it is a fiction to believe that justification does not relate us to the rule of Christ as Lord or that the judgment does not relate us to the work of Christ as Savior. . . . When the end comes, the judgment assesses and testifies to the reality of justification evidenced by the faithful witness of God's people. *In*

*this flow, justification and the judgment do not stand in the relation of tension or contradiction, but in that of inauguration and consummation.*[3]

## Assurance and the last judgment

Judgment according to works does not mean salvation on the basis of works or law observance. The forgiven believer has the confident hope of final salvation. This is Paul's teaching in Romans 5. He wrote: "Since we have been justified through faith, *we have peace with God through our Lord Jesus Christ, through whom we have gained access by faith into this grace in which we now stand. And we rejoice in the hope of the glory of God"* (Rom. 5:1, 2, emphasis added).

Paul based our certainty of future salvation on the reality of our present salvation, the certainty of our future justification on the reality of our present justification: "Since we have now been justified by his blood, *how much the more shall we be saved from God's wrath through him!"* (Rom. 5:9, emphasis added; see also verse 17). In other words, when Jesus justifies us, we have full assurance that He will justify us in the final judgment if we remain in Him. The grace of God reigns not only now but *also* in the last judgment for those who are in Jesus: "so that, just as sin reigned in death, so *also* grace might reign through righteousness to bring eternal life through Jesus Christ our Lord" (Rom. 5:21, emphasis added).

Paul assured redeemed Christians: "There is now no condemnation for those who are in Christ Jesus" (Rom. 8:1). He explained that God has set the believer in Jesus free, because He "condemned sin in sinful man" in the life and death of His own Son (Rom. 8:3). Paul continued this theme of assurance of salvation with these important words that point forward to the last judgment scene:

Who will bring any charge against those whom God has chosen? It is God who justifies. Who is he that condemns? Christ Jesus, who died—more than that, who was raised to life—is at the right hand of God and is also interceding for us. Who shall separate us from the love of Christ? (Rom. 8:33-35).

Paul linked God's act of justification and Jesus' intercession not merely for the present but also for the future judgment. The Messianic prophecies of Isaiah 50:8, 9 and 53:11, 12 placed divine vindication in opposition to condemnation in the believer's experience now. Paul applied their fulfillment to the future judgment as well, using the future tense in Romans 8:33-35. He stated that Jesus' death and resurrection constitute the ground for God's final justification of believers (see also Rom. 5:9, 10). Whoever dares to accuse and condemn them then will have to face God and Christ! Paul implied that neither our sins nor our shortcomings will accuse or condemn us, on the one hand, nor will our moral perfection justify us on the other.

Paul didn't ask what could accuse or condemn the chosen ones but who will bring any charge, who will condemn. He didn't answer that the faith or the moral righteousness of Christians will justify them. He pointed exclusively to God as the source of their justification and to Jesus who will intercede for them. The ground for the believers' final justification and vindication does not lie in their moral achievements but in what God and Jesus have done on their behalf. Paul found these divine acts to provide absolute certainty. *Nothing* can separate believers from the love of God and Christ—nothing in the present or in the future (see Rom. 8:38, 39). Paul was so certain of the believers' final acquittal in the judgment that he declared "those he justified, he also glorified!" (Rom. 8:30). This expresses the ultimate certainty of salvation for true believers.

Because we can never in this life equal Jesus' example of sinless perfection—even though we reflect it in a Christlike character—we still need divine mercy in the final reckoning. We may look forward to that moment of truth with complete confidence, however, because "Jesus Christ is the same yesterday and today and forever" (Heb. 13:8). Ellen White counseled us, "We are not to be anxious about what Christ and God think of us, but about what God thinks of Christ, our Substitute. Ye are accepted in the Beloved."[4] This attitude counts also for the final judgment and motivates us to praise and worship God as our Creator and Redeemer and to join the fervent doxology of all creation:

"To him who sits on the throne and to the Lamb
be praise and honor and glory and power,
for ever and ever!" (Rev. 5:13).

No matter how much good we may have accomplished for the honor and glory of God and for the well-being of humankind, our ultimate confession must be: "By the grace of God I am what I am, and his grace to me was not without effect . . . yet not I, but the grace of God that was with me" (1 Cor. 15:10; compare John 15:5). The redeemed will not boast of their worthiness but rather sing the sevenfold praise of Christ: " 'Worthy is the Lamb, who was slain, to receive power and wealth and wisdom and strength and honor and glory and praise!' " (Rev. 5:12). They realize with never-ending amazement that they owe everything to the free and sovereign grace of God.

Can anyone explain the mercy of God in the final judgment? God has exposed all men as sinners through His law and through the atoning sacrifice of His Son

so that He may have mercy on them all. Oh, the depth of the riches of the wisdom and the knowledge of God! How unsearchable his judgments, and his paths beyond tracing out! . . . "Who has ever given to God, that God should repay him?" For from him and through him and to him are all things. To him be the glory forever! Amen (Rom. 11:32-36).

---

1. E. G. White, *Faith and Works*, 66.

2. G. C. Berkouwer, *Geloof en Rechtvaardiging* (Kampen: Kok, 1949), 108; my translation.

3. Ivan T. Blazen, "Justification and Judgment," *70 Weeks, Leviticus, Nature of Prophecy*, Daniel and Revelation Commentary Series, F. B. Holbrook, ed. (Washington, D.C.: Biblical Research Institute, 1986), 3:343, 344, emphasis added.

4. E. G. White, *Selected Messages*, 2:32, 33.

# Chapter 11

# God's Assurances in Baptism and the Lord's Supper

In addition to His written Word, God's infinite mercy has moved Him to speak to us through some concrete symbols that serve as sacred ordinances. He intends these ordinances, called in church tradition "sacraments," to confirm and to seal His promises in our hearts by the working of the Holy Spirit. The biblical sacraments do not function redemptively independent of God's Word. Instead, they presuppose faith in the written Word. They assure us that God is faithful to His promises, and thereby they strengthen and increase our faith.

Historically, Protestantism and Roman Catholicism differ fundamentally on the number and understanding of the sacraments, as their respective catechisms testify. The Roman Catholic Church recognizes seven sacraments. It teaches that "a sacrament is a visible sign of an invisible grace, instituted for our justification."[1] Remarkably, the Council of Trent decreed that a sacrament is a ritual that is effective *by itself* and bestows the grace of God *ex opere operato*— that is, "on account of the work which is done," if no actual intention to sin is present.[2]

The Protestant creeds acknowledge only two sacraments in the New Testament: baptism and the Lord's Supper. The Heidelberg Catechism of 1563 explains the sacraments as follows:

They are visible, holy signs and seals instituted by God in order that by their use he may the more fully disclose and seal to us the promise of the gospel, namely, that because of the one sacrifice of Christ accomplished on the cross he graciously grants us the forgiveness of sins and eternal life.[3]

The Protestant definition of a biblical sacrament contains three essential points: (1) It is instituted by God and sanctioned by Christ in Scripture. (2) It is an outward symbol or sign of Christ's sanctifying presence that strengthens our faith. (3) It requires one to have faith in the gospel to participate in its promised blessings.

The New Testament links the sacred ordinances indissolubly with the gospel and its promises of salvation. The sacraments do not function spiritually when they are divorced from faith in the promises. In 1 Corinthians 10:1-12 Paul taught this view of the sacraments. There he compared the function of the old covenant sacraments with those of the new covenant. He noted that Israel enjoyed a baptism "into Moses" and ate spiritual food and drank spiritual drink. "Nevertheless," he wrote, "God was not pleased with most of them; their bodies were scattered over the desert" (see 1 Cor. 10:1-5). Partaking of the sacraments did not save their souls or prevent unbelief and apostasy.

So it is with the sacraments of the church! "Now these things occurred as examples to keep us from setting our hearts on evil things as they did" (v. 6). Paul admonished the Christians in Corinth not to misuse the sacraments of baptism and the Lord's Supper by considering them effective for salvation in themselves. Israel had disconnected their sacraments from the obedience of faith, which the old covenant required. Paul saw the same danger threatening the church: "These things happened to them as examples and were written down as warnings for us" (1 Cor. 10:11).

## The biblical meaning of Christian baptism

Christian baptism supersedes the baptism of John the Baptist, promising the gift of the Spirit of God. Jesus linked water baptism and Spirit baptism when He told Nicodemus, " 'No one can enter the kingdom of God unless he is born of water and the Spirit' " (John 3:5). Jesus received both when He was baptized (Matt. 3:16). His anointing by the Spirit fulfilled the Messianic prophecies that the

King-Messiah would be anointed with the fullness of God's Spirit (see Isa. 11:2) and would introduce the age of the outpouring of that Spirit (see Joel 2:28, 29).

On the day of Pentecost, Peter offered all who believe in Jesus the baptism of the Spirit of God *together with* their water baptism (Acts 2:38). Paul confirmed this link by declaring that all who are justified by faith in Jesus have also received the outpouring of God's love in their hearts "by the Holy Spirit" (Rom. 5:5). He insisted that those in Ephesus who were baptized only with water should now be baptized into the name of the Lord Jesus, with the consequence that the Spirit descended upon them (see Acts 19:1-6). This event demonstrated that in the apostolic church Christian baptism was inseparably connected with Spirit baptism. This connection implies that divine forgiveness of our sins includes the gift of the Holy Spirit in water baptism. Paul summed it up this way:

He saved us through the washing of rebirth and renewal by the Holy Spirit whom He poured out on us generously through Jesus Christ our Savior, so that, having been justified by his grace, we might become heirs having the hope of eternal life (Titus 3:5-8).

It was this union of forgiveness and the Holy Spirit that put the element of newness in the "new covenant" the Old Testament promised (see Ezek. 36:24-27). The risen Christ offers us these two gifts from God on the condition that we believe that He is the Son of God (see John 1:33; Gal. 3:2, 5; Titus 3:4-7).

Nowhere can we find a deeper explanation of the theological meaning of baptism than in the following classical passage written by the apostle Paul:

Don't you know that all of us who were baptized into Christ Jesus were baptized into his death? We were therefore buried with him through baptism into death in order that, just as Christ was raised from the dead through the glory of the Father, we too may live a new life. If we have been united with him like this in his death, we will certainly also be united with him in his resurrection (Rom. 6:3-5).

This passage requires a careful understanding of its reasoning. It goes beyond the traditional concept of the dedication of the believer's life to Jesus. Paul explained that through this ordinance God gives baptized believers a real participation in Jesus' historical death on the cross! Being baptized "into Christ Jesus" means being "baptized into his death" (Rom. 6:3). Paul clarified: "We were therefore buried with him through baptism into death" (v. 4). Believers enter Jesus' experience on the cross of Calvary in such a real way that God regards them as legally incorporated into His death. Jesus' death becomes the death of repentant sinners in their baptism. This is God's act and gift in baptism. God sets baptized believers free from His condemnation and retributive justice and assures them of eternal life in the resurrection.

Looking back to his own baptism, Paul said: "I have been crucified with Christ and I no longer live, but Christ lives in me" (Gal. 2:20). He was not speaking of a daily dying to sin but of his *once for all* dying to his sin in his baptism. He expressed this also when he declared: "We are convinced that one died for all, *and therefore all died*" (2 Cor. 5:14, emphasis supplied). William G. Johnsson explains Paul's theology of baptism this way:

> It also signifies our participation in His [Jesus'] death, our incorporation into the crucifixion of the Lord. *When He died, we died!* Not just in the sense that He died in our place and for the sins of the world, because, says Paul, this incorporation is by baptism. Baptism indicates an identification of the *believer* (not of every person) with the death of Jesus.[4]

God counts baptized believers as having died for their sins in Jesus' death. More than that, He gives them the life-giving Spirit of Christ to rule over the power of sin, because God has placed them under the rule of His beloved Son. Paul declares: "For he has rescued us from the dominion of darkness and brought ["transferred," RSV] us into the kingdom of the Son he loves, in whom we have redemption, the forgiveness of sins" (Col. 1:13, 14).

To this salvation believers respond with "the pledge of a good conscience toward God" (1 Pet. 3:21). Paul counsels baptized Christians: "Count yourselves dead to sin but alive to God in Christ Jesus" (Rom. 6:11). They must exercise their faith in accepting and appropriating Jesus' death and resurrection as God's acts of redemption for them. Since they are in Christ, they've been set free from condemnation, set free to conquer the tyranny of sin and evil (Col. 1:14). They can now live a new life (Rom. 6:4).

Ellen G. White described the significance of baptism as follows:

> As Christians submit to the solemn rite of baptism, He [God] registers the vow that they make to be true to Him. This vow is their oath of allegiance. They are baptized in the name of the Father and the Son and the Holy Spirit. Thus they are united with the three great powers of heaven.[5]

> These candidates have entered into the family of God, and their names are inscribed in the Lamb's book of life.[6]

## The Lord's Supper: Sacrament of reassurance

Jesus instituted the ordinance of the Lord's Supper as a communal meal "in remembrance of me" (Luke 22:19; 1 Cor. 11:24, 25). He stipulated that through it the church should remember His atoning death that established the new covenant of the forgiveness of sins:

> He took bread, gave thanks and broke it, and gave it to them, saying, "This is my body given for you; do this in remembrance of me." In the same way, after the supper he took the cup, saying, "This cup is the new covenant in my blood, which is poured out for you" (Luke 22:19, 20).

> He took the cup, gave thanks and offered it to them, saying, "Drink from it, all of you. This is my blood of the covenant,

which is poured out for many for the forgiveness of sins"
(Matt. 26:27, 28).

As the Passover Feast commemorated Israel's miraculous deliverance from God's judgment on Egypt through the blood of the
Passover lamb (see Exod. 12:27-30, 43-46), so Jesus ordained that
the Lord's Supper commemorate the great deliverance from God's
judgment on sin through His blood, the blood of the Lamb of God.
He explicitly pointed to the shedding of His blood as the fulfillment of the promise of the "new covenant" in Jeremiah 31:31-34.
This covenant context makes it quite clear that Jesus was not speaking of His body and blood as physical substances by themselves
in isolation from His person and self-sacrifice. He spoke of His
body as "given for you" and of His blood as "poured out for you."
Both the "given" and the "poured out" refer directly to His impending death.

Paul attributed the same meaning to the Lord's Supper: "Whenever you eat this bread and drink this cup, you proclaim the Lord's
death until he comes" (1 Cor. 11:26). This, the apostolic interpretation of the Lord's Supper, says that in partaking of the emblems—the
bread and the fruit of the vine—Christians are not merely celebrat-
ing Jesus' life. Rather, they are sharing in the blessing that flows
from His sacrificial death on the cross of Calvary.

Consequently, the Supper can be called the sacrificial meal of
the new covenant—in the sense that it offers the fruit of Jesus' atoning death; the forgiveness of sins. The Communion service represents visibly the essence of the gospel and concentrates it in Jesus'
self-sacrifice. It offers Him and the fruits of His death to believers.
The Supper does not *renew* the sacrifice. Instead, it *applies* and *cel-
ebrates* it.

On the basis of Jesus' death, the church looks forward with absolute confidence to His second coming (see 1 Cor. 11:26). The Lord's
Supper connects the cross and the second advent. The certainty of
Jesus' return rests on His atoning death—so, in the church's celebration of the Lord's Supper it witnesses to its living hope in the second
coming. "It is only because of His death that we can look with joy to

His second coming. His sacrifice is the center of our hope. Upon this we must fix our faith."[7]

### The real presence of Christ in the Lord's Supper

The Protestant Reformers Luther and Calvin rejected both the transubstantiation doctrine regarding the "Eucharist," which the Council of Trent later (1551) decreed, and the abstract symbolism Zwingli taught. They accepted instead Jesus' special presence through the Holy Spirit and communion with Jesus in the Spirit. They taught that in the Lord's Supper Jesus offers His sanctifying presence to all who by faith in His promises partake of the emblems. These Reformers insisted on the unbreakable union of the sacrament and the gospel promise of His abiding presence. They stressed that the "sacraments reassure us of God's promises toward us."[8] Calvin developed the Protestant doctrine of the Lord's Supper the most systematically in his famous *Institutes of the Christian Religion* (1559). There he stated that the glorified Christ remains in heaven, but

> he shows his presence in power and strength, is always among his people, and breathes his life upon them, and lives in them, sustaining them, strengthening, quickening, keeping them unharmed, as if he were present in the body. In short, he feeds his people with his own body, the communion of which he bestows upon them by the power of his Spirit. In this manner, the body and blood of Christ are shown to us in the Sacrament.[9]

Calvin explained that communion with the body, or flesh and blood, of Jesus means having fellowship with His real presence, not just with His gifts. It is the power of the Spirit that enables this communion with Jesus. The Lord's Supper does not give believers a new fellowship that they have not experienced before; rather, it symbolizes, confirms, and strengthens the fellowship they have known.

The Seventh-day Adventist Church views the Lord's Supper in basically the same way as did Calvin. The Statement of Fundamental Beliefs declares:

The Lord's Supper is a participation in the emblems of the body and blood of Jesus as an expression of faith in Him, our Lord and Savior. In this experience of Communion Christ is present to meet and strengthen His people. As we partake, we joyfully proclaim the Lord's death until He comes again (No. 15).

The book *Seventh-day Adventists Believe . . . A Biblical Exposition of 27 Fundamental Doctrines* (Silver Spring, Maryland: General Conference of Seventh-day Adventists, 1988) states:

Since we appropriate the benefits of Christ's atoning sacrifice by faith, the Lord's Supper is much more than a mere memorial meal. Participation in the Communion service means a revitalization of our life through Christ's sustaining power, providing us with life and joy.[10]

To grasp the spiritual significance of the Lord's Supper, we may contemplate the words of Jesus in which He called Himself "the bread of life" even before this phrase was connected with the Supper:

Jesus said to them, "I tell you the truth, unless you eat the flesh of the Son of Man and drink his blood, you have no life in you. Whoever eats my flesh and drinks my blood has eternal life, and I will raise him up at the last day. For my flesh is real food and my blood is real drink. Whoever eats my flesh and drinks my blood, remains in me, and I in him" (John 6:53-56).

Jesus explained that His words had a spiritual meaning and were useless if taken in a literal way: " 'The Spirit gives life; the flesh counts for nothing. The words I have spoken to you are spirit and they are life' " (John 6:63). He taught a deeply spiritual experience with the Lord, a participation with His blood and body. Ellen White described it this way: "We must feed upon Him, receive Him into the heart, so that His life becomes our life. His love, His grace, must be assimilated."[11]

That is our privilege whenever we partake of this ordinance.

---

1. *Catechism of the Council of Trent,* translated by J. A. McHugh and C. J. Callan (Westminster, Maryland: Christian Classics, 1974), 143.

2. Canon 8, "Decree Concerning the Sacraments," 1547; in J. Leith, *Creeds of the Churches* (Atlanta: J. Knox Press, 1977), 426.

3. Question 66 in *Reformed Confessions of the Sixteenth Century*, A. C. Cochrane, ed. (Philadelphia: Westminster Press, 1966), 316.

4. William G. Johnsson, *The Meaning of Christian Baptism* (Nashville, Tenn.: Southern Publishing Assn., 1980), 41, 42.

5. E. G. White, *Evangelism*, 307.

6. E. G. White, Ms. 27½, 1900; quoted in *SDA Bible Commentary,* 6:1075.

7. E. G. White, *The Desire of Ages*, 660.

8. A. E. McGrath, *Christian Theology: An Introduction,* 2nd ed. (Malden, Mass.: Blackwell Pubs., 1997), 508.

9. *Institutes,* bk. IV, ch. 17, sec. 18.

10. *Seventh-day Adventists Believe . . . ,* 200.

11. E. G. White, *The Desire of Ages*, 389.

# Chapter 12

# Witnessing With Assurance

Before we can witness about the Lord, we must know Him personally. And we can become acquainted with Him only when He has first spoken and acted. In other words, God must reveal Himself to us before we can speak of Him to others.

God chose Israel and liberated that nation from the house of bondage in Egypt under Moses and then made it His covenant people, revealing to it His divine plan to restore His kingdom on earth. God's election elevated the Israelites as the living witnesses of the Creator-Redeemer. Through Isaiah the Spirit of prophecy said:

> "You are my witnesses," declares the LORD [YAHWEH], "and my servant whom I have chosen, so that you may know and believe me and understand that I am he. . . . I, even I, am the LORD, and apart from me there is no savior. I have revealed and saved and proclaimed—I, and not some foreign god among you. You are my witnesses," declares the LORD, "that I am God. Yes, and from ancient days I am he. No one can deliver out of my hand. When I act, who can reverse it?" (Isa. 43:10-13).

These challenging words charged Israel with the joyful responsibility of proclaiming the good news that the God of Israel is the sovereign God of history: "How beautiful on the mountains are the feet of those who bring good news, who proclaim peace, who bring good tidings, who proclaim salvation, who say to Zion, 'Your God reigns!' " (Isa. 52:7). Paul read this passage of Isaiah with great interest and concluded: "How can they preach unless they are sent?" (Rom. 10:15). God has not left our witnessing about Him to our spontaneous impulses. Rather, such witnessing constitutes a mission for which God has *sent* His people into the world.

From the very beginning, God called His chosen people to be living witnesses of His grace and holiness. To Abraham He said: " 'I will make you into a great nation and I will bless you; I will make your name great, and you will be a blessing' " (Gen. 12:2). These words show that God links His promise with a responsibility: *receiving a blessing obliges one to be a blessing!* In other words, God does not want us to take His mercies for granted. He rightfully desires to receive the glory and the praise! (see Isa. 43:7, 21).

But God finds His glory in seeking the well-being of all people. His covenant with Abraham embraced all the nations and peoples of the earth (see Gen. 12:3). He "wants all men to be saved and to come to a knowledge of the truth" (1 Tim. 2:4). For that universal outreach God made a covenant with Israel: " 'You yourselves have seen what I did to Egypt, and how I carried you on eagles' wings and brought you to myself. . . . Although the whole world is mine, *you will be for me a kingdom of priests and a holy nation*' " (Exod. 19:4-6, emphasis added). So God set Israel free from bondage as slaves so they could be free for Him! They were called to be "priests"; that is, "as intermediaries between God and the heathen, they were to serve as instructors, preachers, and prophets, and were to be examples of holy living—Heaven's exponents of true religion."[1] They were called to be a missionary people, a saving light to the surrounding nations who did not know the living God.

After the Babylonian captivity, God renewed His calling: " 'I will also make you a light for the Gentiles, that you may bring my salvation to the ends of the earth' " (Isa. 49:6). God even invited all the Gentiles to His temple in Jerusalem to worship Him: " 'Foreigners who bind themselves to the LORD to serve him, to love the name of the LORD, and to worship him, all who keep the Sabbath without desecrating it and who hold fast to my covenant—these I will bring to my holy mountain and give them joy in my house of prayer. . . . For my house will be called a house of prayer for all nations' " (Isa. 56:6, 7). Such Gentile worshipers of Yahweh were numbered among spiritual Israel, with "a name better than sons and daughters" (Isa. 56:5).

Ellen G. White wrote an impressive description of this all-embracing outreach of Israel's prophets:

> Heaven's plan of salvation is broad enough to embrace the whole world. God longs to breathe into prostrate humanity the breath of life. And He will not permit any soul to be disappointed who is sincere in his longing for something higher and nobler than anything the world can offer. Constantly He is sending His angels to those who, while surrounded by circumstances the most discouraging, pray in faith for some power higher than themselves to take possession of them and bring deliverance and peace.[2]

## Jesus' call to be His witnesses

When Jesus had completed His mission on earth, He gave His disciples a wonderful promise and an abiding responsibility:

> "You will receive power when the Holy Spirit comes on you: and you will be my witnesses in Jerusalem, and in all Judea and Samaria, and to the ends of the earth" (Acts 1:8).

Jesus called His followers to something more than being "Jehovah's witnesses," as the old-covenant Israelites were. Christians are to be a new-covenant people who recognize the divine Messiah! Jesus made this clear to the Jews: " 'The Father judges no one, but has entrusted all judgment to the Son, *that all may honor the Son just as they honor the Father. He who does not honor the Son does not honor the Father, who sent him' "* (John 5:22, 23). We hear in the book of Revelation that "every creature in heaven and on earth and under the earth [the dead]" will worship both the Father and the Son with equal honor and praise for ever and ever (see Rev. 5:13). Recognizing Jesus Christ as the unique Son of God is absolutely essential to our saving experience, to our assurance for the future, and to our effective witness in the world.

To understand the far-reaching consequences of Jesus' redemptive work for humankind, we must consider His Messianic claims. When He said " 'I am the light of the world' " (John 8:12), He claimed to be the historical fulfillment of the saving presence of Israel's God, Yahweh: "The LORD [YAHWEH] is my light and my salvation—whom shall I fear? The LORD is the stronghold of my life—of whom shall I be afraid?" (Ps. 27:1). Jesus claimed to be the saving and sanctifying "light" for all people in the world! That is more than a doctrine or confession of faith. For King David, it brought the assurance of God's presence, and so to us Jesus as the "Light" provides our assurance of His saving presence. We must experience this personally; then the conviction of our hearts will overflow in a joyful testimony. When Jesus gives new meaning to our life and satisfies the deepest longings of our soul, we will naturally desire to share such a wonderful experience with others. Someone has said that everyone who is born into the kingdom of God is born a missionary. Salvation is not a private matter.

When an Israelite was delivered from illness or the threat of death, he went to the sanctuary of God and invited all people to hear his testimony of how God had answered his prayers: "I will declare your name to my brothers; in the congregation I will praise you" (Ps. 22:23). "I waited patiently for the LORD; he turned to me and heard my cry. He lifted me out of the slimy pit, out of the mud and mire; he set my feet on a rock and gave me a firm place to stand. He put a new song in my mouth, a hymn of praise to our God. Many will see and fear and put their trust in the LORD" (Ps. 40:1-3).

That kind of witness to God's grace is extended in the Christian faith and experience. When Jesus had healed a demon-possessed man, He urged him: " 'Go home to your family and tell them how much the Lord has done for you, and how he has had mercy on you' " (Mark 5:19). This man could witness about Jesus with full assurance because he had felt the Lord's redeeming power. The joy of deliverance from evil motivated his testimony. The receiver became the giver!

Jesus explained the powerful source of the Christian's witness when, on the last day of the Feast of Tabernacles in Jerusalem, He said:

"If anyone is thirsty, let him come to me and drink. *Whoever believes in me,* as the Scripture has said, *streams of living water will flow from within him*" (John 7:37, 38, emphasis added).

Jesus' statement to the Samaritan woman throws light on this saying: " 'Whoever drinks the water I give him will never thirst. *Indeed, the water I give him will become in him a spring of water welling up to eternal life'* " (John 4:14, emphasis added). In both situations Jesus spoke of the Holy Spirit as a powerful assurance and never-ending love in those who believe in Him. He insisted that His disciples wait for this baptism of the Spirit *before* they testified of Him as His witnesses (see Acts 1:5, 8). Only when believers have experienced the baptism of the Spirit of Christ will they bring a Christ-centered and not a pious, ego-centered testimony.

On the day of Pentecost, the apostles declared "the wonders of God" as fulfilled in Jesus. Their witness to the risen Lord was an effective testimony that led many to repentance. Peter promised that all who believed in Jesus and were baptized in His name would receive the gift of the Holy Spirit (Acts 2:38, 39). Because of the convincing witness of the Spirit-filled apostles, about three thousand people became followers of Jesus that day (Acts 2:41).

## The essence of discipleship: salt and light

Jesus' concern extended beyond the intellectual faith of His disciples to their living a new life that blessed others. It is said of Him that "from His earliest years He was possessed of one purpose; He lived to bless others."[3] Jesus was the saving and sanctifying light of the world. He called His disciples to a similar task: " 'You are the salt of the earth. . . . You are the light of the world. A city on a hill cannot be hidden. . . . Let your light shine before men, that they may see your good deeds and praise your Father in heaven' " (Matt. 5:13, 14, 16).

Jesus did not suggest that His disciples could be such a blessing independent of Him. He taught: " 'I am the vine; you are the branches. If a man remains in me and I in him, he will bear much fruit; apart from me you can do nothing' " (John 15:5). Only in intimate connection with Him can the Christian be a light and salt to others. No disciples can ever become another Christ, but disciples can be Christlike! No one can equal the Pattern, but Christians can resemble it according to the ability that God has given.

As Jesus reflected the character of God's holy love perfectly, so His disciples may reflect Jesus' character of self-sacrificing love to others. Jesus summed it up by saying: " 'Be perfect, therefore, as your heavenly Father is perfect' " (Matt. 5:48). The context points out that the character perfection He taught exceeded the legalistic righteousness that His contemporary Pharisees sought through their law observance (see Matt. 5:20). The righteousness or character perfection Jesus prescribed meant reflecting the forgiving and merciful love of God as manifested to His enemies on earth (see Matt. 5:43-48). "We are to be centers of light and blessing to our little circle, even as He is to the universe. We have nothing of ourselves, but the light of His love shines upon us, and we are to reflect its brightness."[4] Jesus summoned His followers to manifest perfect love to all who are hostile to God and His people. So the ideal of a Christian character is Christlikeness.

As salt is vitally important for everyday life, so are Jesus' disciples vitally necessary to the world in their witness to God and His kingdom. They represent to the world the truth of the salvation that has come in Christ Jesus, "the light of the gospel of the glory of Christ" (2 Cor. 4:4). They are called in a "depraved generation" to "shine like stars in the universe as you hold out the word of life" (Phil. 2:15, 16). Without them, the world would be left in darkness. Their presence and testimony becomes the world's only hope. They must now "let their light shine before men" (Matt. 5:16). Donald A. Hagner rightly comments: "Their mission is accomplished, however, not only in word . . . but in the deeds of their daily existence. . . . They are shown [in Matt. 5-7] to be nothing other than the faithful living out of the commandments,

the righteousness of the Torah as interpreted by Jesus."[5]

Peter indicated that our behavior influences people around us and can point them to Jesus. He told Christian women that they can witness to their unbelieving husbands "without words." "They may be won over . . . when they see the purity and reverence of your lives" (1 Pet. 3:1, 2). He admonished the wealthy women in the church not to stress outward appearance but to develop the inward beauty of a gentle spirit: "It should be that of your inner self, the unfading beauty of a gentle and quiet spirit, which is of great worth in God's sight" (1 Pet. 3:4). These are the spiritual qualities that Jesus also possessed (see Matt. 11:29; 21:5).

## Witnessing in the book of Revelation

To give the ultimate witness for Jesus by laying down one's life requires complete assurance of faith. Soon after the first century, the Greek word for "witness," *martys*, came to mean "martyr," because so many Christian witnesses died a martyr's death. To the church in Smyrna, the risen Lord gave this comfort:

> "Be faithful, even to the point of death, and I will give you the crown of life" (Rev. 2:10).

And He acknowledged the faithful witness of the church in Pergamum:

> "I know where you live—where Satan has his throne. Yet you remain true to my name. You did not renounce your faith in me, even in the days of Antipas, my faithful witness, who was put to death in your city—where Satan lives" (Rev. 2:13).

During the reign of Emperor Marcus Aurelius (A.D. 161-180), a great number of Christians suffered cruel punishments, among whom was Polycarp, the old bishop of Smyrna. The proconsul Herod asked him, "What harm is it to say, 'Lord Caesar,' and to sacrifice, and save yourself?" Then he urged the bishop to curse Christ. Polycarp answered, "Eighty-six years have I served him, and he never once wronged me; how then shall I blaspheme my King, who has saved me? . . . I am a Christian—and if you desire to learn the Christian doctrine, assign me a day, and you shall hear."[6] Polycarp was burned alive after he offered this prayer: "O Father, I bless thee that thou hast counted me worthy to receive my portion among the number of martyrs."[7] He died in full assurance of faith. Many more stories could be told about the heroic faithfulness of those who witnessed for Jesus during the time of the Roman Empire and during the dark Middle Ages.

John's Apocalypse stresses two particular characteristics of Jesus' true witnesses by repeating these characteristics seven times with some slight variations (in chapters 1:2, 9; 6:9; 12:17; 14:12; 19:10; 20:4). These characteristics are faithfulness to the Word of God and to the testimony of Jesus. The Christian witnesses were prepared to lay down their lives for this twofold revelation of God and of His Son. John himself was banished to Patmos "because of the word of God and the testimony of Jesus" (Rev. 1:9). Many exegetical scholars understand the genitive expressions "of God" and "of Jesus" in the book of Revelation as subjective genitives—that is, as self-revelations of God and of Jesus to the church. The testimony of Jesus subjected Israel to the ultimate test of faith in the progressive revelation of God's word (see John 3:31, 32). And God's expanded testimony places Israel and the church under the authority of God's Son (see also Heb. 1:1, 2; 2:1-4; 10:26-31; 12:22-29).

The book of Revelation confronts the church with the prospect of severe persecutions (see Rev. 11). Many Christian believers would be brought before human courts, condemned, and executed. For this reason Jesus encourages them to *hold fast* to the "testimony of Jesus," just as He had witnessed faithfully before the Roman governor Pontius Pilate (see 1 Tim. 6:12-14; Rev. 1:5, 9; 2:25; 3:11). The question is, For what kind of "testimony" of Jesus were the faithful ones in church history willing to sacrifice their lives? The content of this testimony of Jesus was His specific teachings—that is, the eternal gospel of His death and resurrection (Rev. 1:18). The New Testament contains the canonical testimonies of the Spirit. And the book of the Revelation of Jesus Christ itself is a constitutive part of His testimony to the churches (Rev. 1:2; 22:16). For this testimony of Jesus John suffered on Patmos (Rev. 1:9) and countless martyrs gave their lives (Rev. 6:9). Ellen White confirmed:

Century after century the blood of the saints had been shed. While the Waldenses laid down their lives upon the mountains of Piedmont "for the word of God, and for the testimony of Jesus Christ," similar witness to the truth had been borne by their brethren, the Albigenses of France.[8]

The remnant church will faithfully maintain this testimony of Jesus in the final conflict with the antichrist, even when they are threatened with a death decree (Rev. 12:17; 20:4).

1. *SDA Bible Commentary,* 1:595.

2. E. G. White, *Prophets and Kings,* 378.

3. E. G. White, *The Desire of Ages,* 70.

4. E. G. White, *Thoughts From the Mount of Blessing,* 77.

5. Donald A. Hagner, *Matthew 1-13.* Word Biblical Commentary 33A (Dallas, Tex.: Word Books, 1993), 102.

6. See the whole account in Foxe's *Book of Martyrs,* W. G. Berry, ed. (Grand Rapids, Mich.: Baker Book House, 1995), 21-23.

7. Ibid., 24.

8. E. G. White, *The Great Controversy,* 271.

# Chapter 13

# Blessed Assurances in the Book of Revelation

John's Apocalypse gives more assurances of life eternal for persevering believers than does any other book in the New Testament. These assurances are concentrated in seven pronouncements of blessing that give structure to the entire book and provide the theme of perfect assurance for the followers of Jesus.

It is no coincidence that the Apocalypse contains exactly seven beatitudes. Ever since Moses' narrative pictured the creation of the world in six days followed by God's rest on the seventh, the number seven has represented fullness, completeness, and perfection. Yahweh promised Cain a "sevenfold" or complete vengeance (Gen. 4:15, 24). The seven sprinklings of the atoning blood brought Israel a complete cleansing (Lev. 16:14, 19). God sees everything in the world with seven eyes (Zech. 4:10). In the kingdom of God the sun will shine "seven times brighter, like the light of seven full days" (Isa. 30:26).

In the New Testament, possession by seven demons represented total possession (Luke 8:2; Matt. 13:43-45). When Jesus told Peter that he should forgive his brother not just seven times but " 'seventy times seven' " (Matt. 18:21, 22), He meant totally and without limit (see also Luke 17:4). Matthew even used the number seven as a "stylistic expression of his theology of fulfillment."[1] The apostle John, however, used the number seven even more than the other authors of the New Testament. He directed his Apocalypse to seven churches in the Roman province of Asia—that is, to all churches (1:4, 11)—and based the very structure of Revelation upon this number.

The Apocalypse's seven beatitudes intend to bring full assurance and hope to God's oppressed people that He will safely guide them to the Promised Land and will fully vindicate them in the last day. Gosnell Yorke observed that "these seven beatitudes are situated at significant points in the sequence of the end-time or eschatological events, taking us from the present and passing period of paradise lost to that future and unending period of paradise regained."[2]

The book of Revelation provides our greatest encouragement to persevere in the faith in spite of adverse circumstances, and the seven beatitudes may be seen as the essence of this book. A study of these specific assurances from Jesus brings a sanctifying power to our hearts and lives. It also directs our hope to the certainty of redemption and salvation in the world to come! "Believers . . . will be given such glimpses of the open gates of heaven that heart and mind will be impressed with the character that all must develop in order to realize the blessedness which is to be the reward of the pure in heart."[3]

## Blessed are those who read, hear, and take to heart

"Blessed is the one who reads the words of this prophecy, and blessed are those who hear it and take to heart what is written in it, because the time is near" (Rev. 1:3).

John's Apocalypse promises a blessing or spiritual benefit in connection with the divine revelation of Jesus Christ, which God had given Him to show His servants "what must soon take place" (Rev. 1:1). This chain of revelation claims that John's Apocalypse speaks with divine authority and has universal validity for all Christians. The book is called a "prophecy" (1:3) from the God of Israel—therefore, it claims authoritativeness; it is to be read publicly, together with the writings of the Old Testament, in the church service (1 Tim. 4:13).

Jesus not only rebukes the lukewarm members and announces His wrath against the impenitent, but He also pronounces a blessing on the readers and hearers of this prophetic book. However, He does not offer this blessing unconditionally. The leaders of the churches are commissioned to read the book aloud in the churches (Rev. 1:3, NRSV; 1:16, 20), and the hearers are to take to heart and to keep what is written in it. This means that merely reading or hearing it will not suffice. The test is in heeding its counsels in practical Christianity.

What needs to be heeded is twofold in nature: "the word [or "commandments"] of God and the testimony [or "faith"] of Jesus" (see Rev. 1:2, 9; 6:9; 12:17; 14:12; 20:4). These statements of John that make the revelation of God twofold equate the testimony of Jesus in the New Testament with the word of God in the Old Testament. Revelation claims that Jesus spoke with the fullness of the Spirit of prophecy (see Rev. 2:1, 7; 19:10; cp. John 3:31-34; Heb. 1:1, 2). Consequently, the Hebrew faith advances, becoming Christian faith!

Paul was not ashamed to die for "the testimony of our Lord" (2 Tim. 1:8, NASB). For this "testimony of Jesus" John was banished to the isle of Patmos (Rev. 1:9) and countless martyrs have sacrificed their lives (Rev. 6:9; 20:4). Faithfulness to the Bible and the Bible alone as the ultimate norm of truth for salvation will also distinguish the last generation of Jesus' followers (see Rev. 12:17; 14:12). Ellen White explained: "God will have a people upon the earth to maintain the Bible, and the Bible only, as the standard of all doctrines and the basis of all reforms."[4]

The psalmist announced: "Blessed are they whose ways are blameless, who walk according to the law of the LORD . . . and seek him with all their heart" (Ps. 119:1).

### Blessed are those who die in the Lord

"Then I heard a voice from heaven say, 'Write: Blessed are the dead who die in the Lord from now on.' 'Yes,' says the Spirit, 'they will rest from their labor, for their deeds will follow them' " (Rev. 14:13).

John placed this beatitude at a significant point in the forecast of end-time events. It is located in the unit of chapters 12–14, near the end of the Christian age, which concludes with Jesus' second advent (Rev.14:14-20). The context indicates that the blessing is not pronounced on the dead in general but on those who die "in the Lord" during the final crisis of faith. The expression "from now on" has a special meaning in this end-time setting when the antichrist will per-

important

secute all who refuse to bow before the "image of the beast" (Rev. 13:11-17). The saints choose to obey the threefold angels' message that honors the commandments of God and the faith of Jesus (Rev. 14:12). They have the divine assurance that their acts are recognized in heaven and will be rewarded by the grace of God.

Ellen White described the essence of the final crisis:

> Those who keep the commandments of God and the faith of Jesus [14:12] will feel the ire of the dragon and his hosts. Satan numbers the world as his subjects; he has gained control of the apostate churches; but here is a little company that are resisting his supremacy. If he could blot them from the earth, his triumph would be complete. As he influenced the heathen nations to destroy Israel, so in the near future he will stir up the wicked powers of earth to destroy the people of God. All will be required to render obedience to human edicts in violation of the divine law.[5]

The beatitude of Revelation 14:13 brings comfort to all who die in the Lord Jesus, as Paul assured in 1 Thessalonians 4:13-18 and in 1 Corinthians 15:51-57. But the pronouncement of blessing in Revelation 14 applies with peculiar force to the last generation of Jesus' people.

## Blessed is he who stays awake and is clothed

" 'Behold, I come like a thief! Blessed is he who stays awake and keeps his clothes with him, so that he may not go naked and be shamefully exposed' " (Rev. 16:15).

Some Bible versions (NRSV, NASB) have placed this verse in parentheses, as if it is out of order here. But this devalues the special function this beatitude has in the end-time setting of the seven last plagues (described in chapters 15 and 16). This beatitude reaches beyond the previous one, placing us in the time *after* human probation has closed (see Rev. 15:5-8). Situated between the sixth and the seventh plagues, it comes at the moment of the destruction of worldwide Babylon (Rev. 16:17-21). It is placed there as a warning for the saints not to fall asleep in false security but to *remain* in fellowship with Jesus. The prophets knew that God alone can provide "the garments of salvation," the "robe of righteousness" (Isa. 61:10; Zech. 3).

To face Jesus in His glory, each saint must be clothed in the robe of His righteousness. Jesus offers it now, as we hear from His words to the church in Laodicea: " 'I counsel you to buy from me gold refined in the fire, so you can become rich; *and white clothes to wear, so you can cover your shameful nakedness' "* (Rev. 3:18, emphasis added). In his first letter to the churches, the apostle John wrote: "And now, dear children, continue in him [Jesus], so that when he appears we may be confident and unashamed before him at his coming" (1 John 2:28). This explains the staying awake and being clothed as meaning to "continue," or to abide, in Jesus. Earlier, using the illustration of a vine and its branches, Jesus had counseled, " 'Remain in me, and I will remain in you' " (John 15:4).

The beatitude in Revelation 16:15 corresponds with Jesus' counsel to the church in Laodicea in chapter 3:18. Both speak of "clothes" that cover our nakedness and shamefulness. While in that earlier passage the Lord urges us to receive *His* robe of righteousness in the present time, in Revelation 16 He warns us that we cannot stand in the day of His wrath without His protection. Therefore, we must come to Him in earnest repentance (see Rev. 3:19). Only His gift of righteousness will prepare believers for His return, when He comes unexpectedly, "like a thief" in the night. Jesus also warned that before His wedding banquet begins He will look for the gift of His wedding clothes (see Matt. 22:11).

### Blessed are those who are invited to Jesus' wedding banquet

*"Then the angel said to me, 'Write: "Blessed are those who are invited to the wedding supper of the Lamb!" ' And he added, 'These are the true words of God' " (Rev. 19:9).*

On one occasion when Jesus was a supper guest, He heard someone exclaim, " 'Blessed is the man who will eat at the feast in the kingdom of God' " (Luke 14:15). Jesus responded by telling a parable of a great banquet. He said that the host sent notices to all who had been invited, saying, " 'Come, for everything is now ready' " (Luke 14:17). However, the invitees all made excuses. Only strangers, the poor, and the handicapped came to the banquet. Jesus concluded His story with this prophetic warning: " 'I tell you, not one of those men who were invited will get a taste of *my* banquet' " (Luke 14:24, emphasis added). Jesus predicted that many Gentiles would accept Him as the Messiah of prophecy: " 'I say to you that many will come from the east and the west, and will take their [Israel's] places at the feast with Abraham, Isaac and Jacob in the kingdom of heaven' " (Matt. 8:11).

Revelation 19 says this wedding banquet of the Lamb will be held *in heaven*, after Jesus' second coming. It places this banquet in direct contrast with "the great supper of God," in which all the rebellious wicked and their religious leaders are consumed by the glory of the returning Christ (see Rev. 19:17-21). It is essential for our sense of assurance that the angel added to his beatitude: " 'These are true words of God' " (Rev. 19:9, NRSV). No greater assurance can be given us!

The fourth beatitude leads us into the heavenly places where the angels, the elders, and the living creatures shout four "Hallelujahs" (Rev. 19:1-6), which remind us of the "Hallel" or praise psalms in Psalms 113–118, sung at Israel's Passover. All heaven shouts for joy because God has finally meted out justice on the persecuting "harlot," avenged the blood of His servants (verse 2), and destroyed Babylon (verse 3). And in "the song of the Lamb," the glorified saints sing praises to their divine Redeemer (Rev. 15:2-4). Ellen White described this impressively:

> When the earthly warfare is accomplished, and the saints are all gathered home, our first theme will be the song of Moses, the servant of God. The second theme will be the song of the Lamb, the song of grace and redemption. This song will be louder, loftier, and in sublimer strains, echoing and re-echoing through the heavenly courts.[6]

In this apocalyptic perspective, the glorified saints are the guests of the wedding supper, while the bride is "the New Jerusalem"—the holy city in which the saints will dwell forever together with God Almighty and the Lamb! (See Rev. 21:2, 9, 10, 22, 27.) There can be no separation between the "guests" and the "bride"; both symbols merge. Alan F. Johnson comments:

> The time of betrothal has ended. Now it is the time for the church, prepared by loyalty and suffering, to enter into her full experience of salvation and glory with her beloved spouse, Christ. The fuller revelation of the realization of this union is described in chapters 21 and 22.[7]

Note the harmony in Revelation 19:7, 8 between God's grace ("fine linen *was given her*") and discipleship ("his bride *made herself ready*").

## Blessed are those who reign in heaven

*"Blessed and holy are those who have part in the first resurrection. The second death has no power over them, but they will be priests of God and of Christ and will reign with him for a thousand years"* (Rev. 20:6).

This text indicates that blessedness, or happiness, and holiness go hand in hand. This is the essence of the redemptive imperative of the gospel of Jesus: " *'Blessed are the pure in heart*, for they will see God' "; "Make every effort to live in peace with all men and to be holy; *without holiness no one will see the Lord*" (Matt. 5:8; Heb. 12:14, emphasis added).

Timewise, the beatitude of Revelation 20 leads us beyond the previous one. It informs us that the saints who will be immortalized by "the first resurrection" will do more than just celebrate and sing in heaven. They will receive a sacred responsibility as "priests and kings" together with Jesus that will last "a thousand years." They are assigned the holy task of being coregents and assessors in the work of judging the impenitent ones, including the fallen angels (see Matt. 19:28; 1 Cor. 6:2, 3).

John wrote: *"I saw thrones on which were seated those who had been given authority to judge.* And I saw the souls of those who had been beheaded *because of their testimony for Jesus and because of the word of God* [literally: *"because of the testimony of Jesus and because of the word of God,"* NASB]" (Rev. 20:4, emphasis added). John's placement of these "thrones" in heaven reveals that they represent a heavenly court, one similar to the one shown to Daniel (see Dan. 7:9, 10, 13, 14). While in Daniel's vision the persecuted saints are judged and vindicated by the divine Judge (Dan. 7:22), in Revelation 20 these faithful saints are enthroned with Jesus and given the authority to judge. "Here is a clear progression in history and indicates that the heavenly court sessions in Dan. 7 and in Rev. 20 succeed each other. . . . The honor from God to reign with Christ is for the overcomers."[8]

## Blessed are those who keep Jesus' testimony and who wash their robes

" *'Behold, I am coming soon! Blessed is he who keeps the words of the prophecy in this book. . . . Blessed are those who wash their robes, that they may have the right to the tree of life, and may go through the gates into the city' " (Rev. 22:7, 14).*

Revelation 22:7-21 brings us back to our present reality and responsibilities. It calls us to partake of a foretaste of the future joys by walking humbly with God and following Jesus. This is expressed in the two final beatitudes, "Blessed is he who keeps the words of the prophecy of this book" (22:7) and "Blessed are those who wash their robes" (22:14). The connection of these two Christian duties teaches that by itself, outward compliance with God's commandments won't guarantee us entrance into the Holy City. Believers also need the continuous cleansing of their souls, symbolically portrayed as the "washing of their robes" (22:14, according to the oldest version).

The key text that explains the meaning of the last beatitude is Revelation 7:14, " *'These are they who have come out of the great tribulation; they have washed their robes and made them white in the blood of the Lamb. Therefore they are before the throne of God' "* (emphasis added). Christians must do this "washing" daily, as indicated by the present tense of the verbal form [*hoi plynôntes*, "those who are washing"]. The washing of our robes in the blood of the Lamb expresses our participation by faith in the atoning blood of Jesus. It means our daily exercise of faith in seeking and accepting the forgiving and sanctifying grace of Jesus, our daily experience of the forgiveness of our guilt and of victory over the power of sin. The blood of the Lamb cleanses our consciences from an evil life (Heb. 9:14). Holiness of life will be the practical line of demarcation between the redeemed and those who must remain "outside" (see Rev. 22:15).

Significantly then, the book that closes the Bible, the book that looks in greatest detail at the times of trouble of the last days, is also a book that focuses on assurance—full assurance that God will safely guide His oppressed people to the Promised Land and will vindicate them in the end. This assurance calls us to hope and to persevere in our faith.

1. E. D. Schmitz, in *The New International Dictionary of the New Testament*, C. Brown, ed. (Grand Rapids, Mich.: Zondervan, 1976), 2:691.

2. Gosnell L. O. R. Yorke, *The Seven Beatitudes of the Book of Revelation* (College Heights, Alberta: Parkland Colorpress, 1985), 8, 9.

3. E. G. White, *Testimonies to Ministers*, 114.

4. E. G. White, *The Great Controversy*, 595.

5. E. G. White, *Testimonies for the Church*, 5:472, 473.

6. E. G. White, *Testimonies for Ministers*, 433.

7. *The Expositor's Bible Commentary* (Grand Rapids, Mich.: Zondervan, 1981), 12:571.

8. H. LaRondelle, *How to Understand the End-Time Prophecies of the Bible* (Sarasota, Fl.: First Impressions, 1997), 460.